Plain Buggies

Amish, Mennonite, and Brethren Horse-Drawn Transportation

by Stephen Scott

a People's Place Booklet

Good Books

Photograph Credits

Cover photos: front—Richard Reinhold; back—Stephen Scott.

All photos throughout the book are by the author Stephen Scott except the following:

John M. Zielinski—5 (top), 8, 31, 37 (center, right) and 74; Richard Reinhold—5 (bottom), 7, 11, 13 (top and bottom), 21, 27 (top), 28 (top and bottom), 29, 30, 37 (bottom), 39 (top and bottom), 41 (top), 42 (both bottom), 50 and 53 (left); David L. Hunsberger (from the book *People Apart)*—10, 84 (bottom right), and 85; Perry Cragg—19, 33 (bottom), and 61; Beth Oberholtzer—27 (bottom); Craig Heisey—34; *The Star News* (Medford, Wisconsin)—75 (bottom); *The Wichita Eagle* and *The Wichita Beacon*—75 (top); Kenneth Pellman—80, 81 (right), and 96; Thomas Anderson—83 (left); Nancy Jo Brown—87; Calvin Redekop—88; *Mennonitische Post*—89 (left and right).

Design, charts, and map by Craig Heisey. Buggy drawings by Stephen Scott.

PLAIN BUGGIES: AMISH, MENNONITE AND BRETHREN HORSE-DRAWN TRANSPORTATION
Copyright © 1981 by Good Books, Lancaster, PA 17602
International Standard Book Number: 0-9346-7202-4
Library of Congress Catalog Card Number 81-82208

Contents

1. Why Horses and Buggies?

Uninformed travelers may be suddenly alarmed if confronted with a horse and buggy traveling down the road driven by a somberly dressed man in a large black hat or a woman wearing a face-concealing bonnet. Has some freakish lapse in time occurred bringing this antique vehicle from a century ago to a modern asphalt road?

If the travelers should inquire locally they would find it was no mirage they saw but flesh and blood people. These are rural folk, the followers of the "Old Order" of their religious heritage; Amish, Mennonite, German Baptist, or River Brethren. They are "plain people" because of their unadorned life style. They are "Pennsylvania Dutch" because they are descended from Germans who settled in Penn's "Holy Experiment" in the eighteenth century.

Do They Like Being "Backward"?

Why do these people insist on retaining a nineteenth century mode of transportation in this supersonic age? Are they a backward primitive tribe or stubborn traditionalists whose reason for everything is, "This is the way we always did it"? Do they just enjoy being odd? Do they feel that automobiles are sinful? Perhaps if you asked the average Old Order person why he drives a horse and buggy he would find it difficult to give you a clear-cut answer. Others have made statements on their beliefs which are quite logical.

The plain people believe that everyday life cannot be separated from religion. Just as magistrates have divine authority to make laws not expressly mentioned in the Bible and parents need no proof texts to back up rules for their children, so the church has the God-given right to set up guidelines for the spiritual welfare of its people. The rules do not replace the Bible but interpret the Bible as the church feels it applies to life today. If anything is a hindrance to the spiritual well-being of the church it should be abstained from.

Horse-drawn vehicles are an increasingly common sight across the United States and Canada. Large Old Order settlements are found in Pennsylvania, Ohio, and Indiana. In the last two decades many new settlements have been started in Missouri, Wisconsin, New York, and even Montana. There are presently Old Order communities in twenty-two states, one Canadian province and four Latin American countries. With large families and the retention of most of their children the Old Orders will probably continue to seek new homelands. They are far from a dying people.

More than 100,000 persons in North America refuse to drive cars for religious reasons (this total includes children). But these communities are dynamic, not static, purposefully charting their life and faith together.

The Problems with Cars

The various groups which retain horse-drawn vehicles believe it is very important to maintain a close-knit family, church, and community structure. It is felt that the auto is a disintegrating force on these institutions. With fast, easy transportation readily available, family members are apt to be away from home more often than not, and the church community is likely to become very scattered. The auto also tends to draw people to the city and the plain people feel that this is no place for a Christian to be. After all, they reason, Lot's downfall was his entrance into the city of Sodom. Abraham remained content tending his sheep and cattle far out on the plain.

Old Orders believe that automobiles in the hands of young people are an especially harmful influence. Lovers' lanes and drive-in theaters are a typical part of automobile courtship.

Those promoting and selling cars emphasize that their product is designed for style, speed, comfort, and convenience. The plain people believe that one should deny one's self of these things as much as possible. A life of luxury is not for the Christian.

Few would dispute that cars are often the objects of pride and ostentation. Humility is a central theme in Old Order doctrine. Certainly followers of Christ would want to avoid status symbols and keeping up with the Joneses.

The Old Orders point out that cars are very expensive and that they tend to bring radios into the church if the owner neglects to remove this harmful device from his car. They also insist that automobiles are dangerous. Who ever heard of loss of life due to two buggies crashing? Of course car-buggy accidents are often fatal to the horse driver but if the Old Order had been driving a car both drivers could have been killed. Would a Christian want to be guilty of sending a sinner to hell, they ask.

A strong point made against the auto is the associated evil of insurance. Many Old Orders avoid liability insurance because they feel it is trusting in man rather than God. Having a written insurance policy would tend to show that a person is expecting something bad to happen. Such a fatalistic attitude is not regarded as scriptural. The Old Orders also wish to avoid an unequal yoke with "worldly" insurance companies who may resort to unchristian tactics to settle a case. In most cases the church district or associated districts help needy members in an unorganized way. In one incident a $10,000 judgment was made against the owner of a buggy involved in a car-buggy accident. The Amish church districts of the area helped pay the amount in full. In some cases, where there is especially heavy car traffic, the Old Orders have resorted to carrying special liability plans of their own or even taking policies from "worldly" companies.

Most Old Order Amish and Mennonites will ride in a car; it is the ownership and driving to which they object. They feel that the automobile is a disintegrating force on close-knit family, church, and community structures.

Some critics point out that many of the evils the Old Orders are trying to avoid by using horses and buggies are very much present with them. The buggy drivers believe things would be much worse if they had cars. The temptations and problems increase in ratio to the speed of the vehicle, it is said.

Do They Ride in Cars?

The Old Orders make much use of public transportation but since connections are often poor they must also depend upon hired cars and vans. The Old Orders do not believe that cars are wrong per se but feel that the automobile breaks up family and community living. They try to control auto usage by forbidding ownership and limiting the use of taxis.

The majority of plain people have no qualms about using public transportation or, if necessary, occasionally paying a neighbor to take them somewhere in a car or van.

A few radicals among the Old Orders try to shun all motor transportation. They have been known to travel hundreds of miles in covered wagons over modern roads. These people feel that the horse is man's God-given mode of transportation and that mechanical locomotion is an act of defiance against God.

As with any rule there are those who go as far as they can. The enforcement of auto usage rules varies greatly from one community to the next.

Groups Split Over Auto

The history of the various Old Order groups follows a general pattern. During the last half of the nineteenth century various influences from the large evangelical denominations affected the "plain churches." The traditionalist insisted that such things as Sunday School, revival meetings, the use of the English language, and, in some cases, the use of meeting-houses, were unnecessary innovations which the church fathers did quite well without. Eventually divisions occurred in which the progressives and conservatives went their separate ways. Those who held firmly to the ancient ways were termed "Old Order," whether Amish, Mennonite, German Baptist, or River Brethren.

During the first decades of the twentieth century a new controversy erupted among the Old Orders. Were the new contrivances called "horseless carriages" proper for plain people to use? At first these machines were very expensive and out of reach for the average farmer. As mass production brought the price down the temptation became greater for the Old Orders. Many church leaders felt that this mode of transportation could be harmful to God's people. Rules were made prohibiting ownership of autos. Throughout the Old Order communities

There are at least ninety different varieties of horse-drawn vehicles among the Amish, Mennonite and Brethren groups of North America. This idyllic scene shows a white and brown Nebraska Amish buggy in central Pennsylvania.

many factions felt that the auto was a useful invention and argued for its acceptance. In time a new series of divisions took place. Some groups wanted to preserve the best of the Old Order traditions but wished to adopt the use of cars. Others joined with the progressives their fathers had parted with a generation or so before.

The divisions began in the 1920's and continued into the 30's. As roads improved and motor transportation became more alluring to Old Orders, divisions increased in the 1940's and 50's. By the 1960's the fragmentation process had slowed down because most communities already had one or more churches formed by modern-minded Old Orders. Few divisions took place in the 1970's. The Old Orders who wished to "go modern" usually had several churches to choose from.

Many individuals and groups leaving the Old Order state that they wish to get away from the spiritual and moral inconsistencies present in many Old Order groups. This is no doubt a sincere motive on the part of many. The Old Orders, however, do not see how driving an automobile relates to being more spiritual. The Old Orders also point out that when cars are accepted the dress of the people involved usually becomes more fashionable and less modest.

Buggies Were Not Always "Backward"

The horse and buggy which is so much a symbol of the nonconformed life to present Old Orders was at one time thought of as an item of luxury. Very few rural people during the eighteenth century had more than crude carts or wagons. Indeed roads in that age were so poor that travel was quite difficult for any vehicle. Wealthy aristocrats had their elaborate carriages, but these were generally limited to city use or on large plantations. The early nineteenth century brought improved roads and trimmer vehicles featuring the newly invented eliptic spring.

The plain people have always been slow to accept new things and continued to walk and ride horseback after various kinds of passenger wagons became common. One can theorize that the first vehicles used by plain people were very simple affairs which were considered obsolete or very unstylish by outsiders.

The general pattern for Old Orders has been to hold off on adopting new things until after the object is very commonplace and no longer thought of as a luxury item. Then a few individuals begin using simple old-fashioned models of the thing which had been under question and gradually the once forbidden item becomes acceptable. This process was no doubt involved in accepting such things as windmills, threshing machines, and even women's shawls and bonnets. The various Old Order groups draw the line at many different places however.

The process of change for Old Order Mennonites is especially well documented through letters and family histories. According to tradition the first Mennonite in the Weaverland area of Lancaster County to use a wheeled vehicle was Christian Zimmerman who was allowed this privilege around 1800 because his excessive weight would not allow him to ride horseback. The custom of young men riding horseback rather than in buggies endured nearly to the end of the century. In 1894 David Burkholder, son of Deacon Daniel S. Burkholder, was given money to buy a saddle on his eighteenth birthday. David refused the gift because all the other young people were now using buggies.

This same Deacon Daniel S. Burkholder (1833-1915) stated that he saw buggy springs create a controversy twice: once when hickory springs were introduced and later when steel springs were first used. Vehicles without tops were permitted first, then simple tops came on the scene. The change from white tops to black tops created a stir among Franconia Conference Mennonites in the 1840's. Buggies with folding tops were strongly discouraged when they were introduced by young men as early as the 1870's. Even thirty years later these vehicles were to be gotten rid of after marriage. Seats with springs were at first considered a luxury. Dashboards were discouraged by Pike Mennonites well into the twentieth century and both Pike and Wenger Mennonites did not commonly have storm fronts until several decades after 1900.

It is doubtful that Old Orders will soon adopt a simple old-fashioned style of automobile. The horse and buggy has become very much an

This barnraising scene near Waterloo, Ontario illustrates many of the characteristics of Old Order life: simple living, modest dress, horse-drawn transportation, mutual aid, and deep religious conviction.

Even children's play utilizes the motifs of horse and buggy. Odd things are odd only to those who are not familiar with them.

integral part of the Old Order way of life. On this and other matters the plain people have said, "Whoa," to change.

An Old Order River Brethren man once designed a very simple truck-like passenger vehicle which he thought would be acceptable for plain people. A manufacturer agreed to produce the body which could be placed on various auto chassis. The church rejected his idea, however. The man did not become offended but remained with the Old Orders until his death.

2. Buggy Use Today

An Old Order child gets his first experience with horses in the field operating various farm implements. Depending upon the maturity of the child he may be allowed to take a buggy out on a back road by age nine. By twelve most children can handle a horse and buggy in any situation. In some communities children get their first driving experience with pony carts.

A Young Man's Buggy

A boy gets a buggy of his own at about age sixteen. If there are a number of teenage boys at home each one will have his own buggy. Single girls generally do not have their own buggies. Young men, especially if they are not yet members of the church, are apt to decorate their vehicles with reflectors, luminous tape, pin striping, decals, and even bumper stickers. The interior may be upholstered wall to wall with fake fur or tiger stripe material and may feature a stereo tape deck with speakers mounted in the corners. Most of this "extravagance" is put away before baptism.

In many communities the young folks have favored or even been restricted to open buggies even though adults could have vehicles with tops. This custom changed early in the twentieth century in La Grange County, Indiana, lasted until the 1940's in Ohio, and was the usual thing among Lancaster Amish youth until quite recently. The Renno Amish young people of Mifflin County, Pennsylvania, still use the open buggy predominantly.

Family Buggies

In a typical large Old Order family a two-seated vehicle serves the parents and small children. An older one-seat buggy, often the one owned by the father in his youth, may be used for occasional errands. One or more single buggies owned by teenage boys may also fill the sheds. These may be used by other members of the family as well.

An open spring wagon serves as a utility vehicle to haul bags of feed and other heavy loads. The "cab wagon," with a top over the front seat and an open bed in back, is used in the same way. Both of these wagons may be fitted with side boards to haul calves or pigs to market. In Pennsylvania the market wagon has a completely enclosed body and in many cases is used as a two-seat vehicle as well as a utility wagon. For light traveling the plain people often make use of two-wheeled carts. Sleighs or bob sleds are usually stored somewhere on an Old Order farm, but with roads being cleared of snow so rapidly today they are rarely used in most areas.

A young man gets a buggy of his own at about age sixteen. In some communities these are open buggies, in others they are top buggies. Taking good care of his buggy is important because sometimes the girls are watching!

These three photos illustrate a wide variety of uses of horse-drawn vehicles: a grocery shopping trip in a Dover, Delaware buggy (top); hauling building supplies in a Lancaster Amish market wagon (note the tailgate); and a New Holland, Pa. Mennonite spring wagon loaded with possessions.

So as many as six different vehicles may be found on a single Old Order farm. This does not include heavy farm wagons not ordinarily used on the road.

Most vehicles used by the plain people are meant to seat either two or four people. In a few instances three-seat six-passenger vehicles are found. Many times vehicles are filled beyond capacity but this means sitting on laps and having little elbow room. Of course children occupy less space and in large families they may be placed in every available corner including the floor.

In many communities of the plain people, local businesses supply hitching rails for their Old Order customers. This family is shopping in Middlefield, Ohio.

Keeping Warm and Dry

A lap robe is often used year-round especially in open buggies. This is mainly to keep the clothes clean since the horse often sheds hair and kicks up mud. In cold weather blankets are piled on and extra heavy clothing is worn. In some cases special propane burning heaters are mounted on the dash. Other methods of keeping warm include hot bricks wrapped in blankets, plastic jugs filled with hot water, and lanterns which radiate a certain amount of heat.

Open buggies are equipped with large black umbrellas, usually stored under the seat. The older style top buggies have roll-down curtains supplemented by a canvas apron which snaps to the buggy box and side

15

Few pictures sum it up like this one.

Are You a Considerate Driver?

Common courtesy on the road can save lives, and very possibly your own. Why is it that it sometimes appears that we as plain people think it is a sign of weakness to be considerate of others on the road?

Although it is really never very safe to drive along busy highways with horse-drawn vehicles, fortunately, there are ways to reduce the danger. Such vehicles should travel as far on the shoulder of the road as possible and if there is room to drive beside the hard surface, so much the better. If it is necessary to travel in the lane of traffic then those who follow should leave a space between each vehicle long enough for a car to get into it at all times. It's a lot easier to pass only one or two buggies than a long string of them. If you drove a car and were in a hurry, how would you feel? Not hard to imagine, is it?

If you think you own half the road and insist on taking up one whole side of the road, then remember who makes the laws and that in most states it is against the law for a slow moving vehicle to hold up the traffic needlessly. If you think you have a right to the road because you pay tax, consider that a large portion of the upkeep expenses for the roads comes from the gasoline tax. A horse does not use much gasoline.

It is our Christian duty to try to keep up the goodwill of those we meet on the road. If we fail to do so, we are neglecting our duty.

Have you ever seen the wave of the hand and the smiles of the motorist after you have given him the all-clear signal when he couldn't quite see over the hill yet? I have and it feels a lot better than to hear the sound of the roaring motor and slipping tires as the exasperated motorist finally pulls around you after having to poke along behind you for some time. This gives you a guilty feeling because you know you have angered someone by sloppy driving, by being rude and inconsiderate.

But just one word of caution, be sure the road is clear before you give the signal to pass.

— **Family Life, January, 1976**

posts. In all the larger communities and many smaller ones, storm fronts, the buggy version of a windshield, give added protection. Sliding doors are also a common feature. All these extras are subject to church rules and may or may not be allowed in individual districts.

In many communities of the plain people local businesses supply hitching rails for their Old Order customers. Some towns provide special parking areas for buggies which may include long open-sided sheds. In Ontario, the towns of Milverton and Elmira have very large barns for horses and buggies to park in. In Millersburg, Ohio the Amish must pay for parking meters along the courthouse hitching rail.

At large gatherings, such as funerals or weddings, young boys serve as hostlers to park the buggies and provide necessary care for the horses. At times buggies are identified with chalk numbers written on the side.

Buggy Etiquette on the Road

Since slow-moving horse-drawn vehicles may be a nuisance to some auto drivers the Old Order people must take special care to stay on the good side of their faster moving fellow travelers. An article in the January, 1976 issue of **Family Life** (an Amish publication) gives some "rules for the road" (see above).

3. Buggy Manufacturing

In the days when buggy manufacturing was a major industry in America many plain people purchased their vehicles from "non-plain" shops. They either chose the simplest styles, had buggies custom-made, or modified the vehicles to their own specifications. A few plain people were involved in buggy-making at an early date like Michael Stoltzfus of Lancaster County who began operating a shop early in this century.

As the twentieth century went into its third decade there were very few buggy makers around, so many plain people began buying up discarded vehicles from their modern neighbors. In fairly recent years buggy dealers have combed through rural areas in Canada, especially Quebec, searching for discarded buggies.

Who Makes Buggies?

Eventually even the relics from the past became scarce and more and more shops producing new buggies and run by Old Order people sprang up. Today most communities with at least two church districts have their own buggy shops. In smaller settlements the people either construct their own buggies or order from larger settlements. Even these small communities have a shop where buggies can be repaired.

The **1977 Old Order Shop and Service Directory** lists over seventy shops involved in some aspect of buggy-making. Since many communities and groups are not included, the actual total may be about 100. Seventeen shops are listed for the Holmes County, Ohio area, ten for Elkhart and La Grange Counties, Indiana, and eleven for Lancaster County, Pennsylvania (not including several Old Order Mennonite shops). Some of these shops are quite large with five or more employees; others are operated part-time by one man. Often they are family-run shops in which the wife and children also help.

Many Shops Needed to Make One Buggy

Very few shops construct a buggy from start to finish. A number of buggy parts require special skill and equipment to produce. Foremost of these items is wheels. A number of shops make wheels only on a large scale; others make only shafts. In many cases one shop will assemble the under carriage which consists of the wheels, axles, springs, and the reaches which connect the two axles. The wooden top part of the buggy will be made at another shop and then the whole buggy is assembled,

Very few shops construct a buggy from start to finish. Today most communities with at least two church districts have their own buggy shops.

Some of these shops are quite large with five and more employees; others are operated part-time by one man. Often they are family-run shops in which the wife and children also help.

painted, and upholstered where the running gear is made.

A number of specialty items and supplies are distributed to buggy shops by parts houses like Witmer's Coach Shop of New Holland, Pennsylvania or Miller's Carriage Company of Shipshewana, Indiana. Such things as springs, axles, fifth wheels (turning devices), door handles, step plates, top fabric, upholstery supplies, mirrors, rubber tires, and electrical supplies and lights are obtained in this way. In turn these items are either manufactured in Old Order shops, or custom-made by modern factories. As much as $600 worth of metal parts may be needed for one buggy.

Buggy Technology Improves

Technological progress in the buggy industry did not stop when it was taken over by the Older Order people. A number of practical improvements are the result of the plain people's ingenuity. A prime example of this is the work of Amishman R. P. Schrock of Holmes County, Ohio. In 1950 Mr. Schrock had representatives from Timken Roller Bearings design a special buggy axle. About twenty buggies were equipped with these axles and sold, but within a short time every last axle broke. Mr. Schrock felt that this failure was due to faulty design and came up with some new ideas of his own and had axles made to his specifications. Before he sold any of these axles he had some installed on a new buggy and had it hauled all over Ohio behind a jeep. The 1036 miles covered represented two years of normal use and included every kind of road and higher speeds than a buggy would ordinarily travel. Schrock's demonstration proved successful and today very few new buggies are produced without roller bearing axles.

In some areas vehicles are equipped with brakes. The older style has a hand lever or foot pedal that operates long arms ending in leather or

A typical Old Order may own no more than three passenger vehicles in his life. Buggies are rarely traded in for newer models since styles change slowly or not at all.

rubber shoes which drag against the steel tire. A recent innovation is the use of hydraulic brakes. The brake drums are attached to the front or back wheel hubs. The brakes are applied with an interior foot pedal. These brakes are becoming increasingly popular and in many communities all new vehicles are equipped with them.

Hard (or solid) rubber tires first came on the American scene in the 1890's. Only a comparatively few groups of plain people ever adopted this feature but some rather large Amish and Mennonite communities have used them for many years.

Battery-operated head and tail lights are used by all but the most conservative Old Orders. These gained acceptance in Lancaster County as early as the 1920's, and just as early by the Mifflin County Renno Amish and the Amish of New Wilmington, Pennsylvania. In Holmes County they began appearing in the 1930's. La Grange County, Indiana Amish did not accept electric buggy lights until much later.

Head lights usually have a high and low beam switch on the floor board. Many buggies also have a dome light. On some Indiana buggies, a light goes on when the boot lid is lifted. The current for these lights is supplied by a storage battery placed under a seat in the rear storage compartment, or suspended on a platform beneath the buggy. A few buggies are equipped with generators or alternators mounted on a wheel, but this pulls harder when charging and many people choose not to give their horse that extra work. Where diesel or gasoline engines are used to supply power for milking equipment or other machinery, battery chargers are operated by each family. In some communities Old Order and "modern" people, as well, make a business of charging batteries. A Lancaster County Amishman has produced a solar charger to be mounted on the carriage roof.

Oak, poplar, and hickory have been the most frequently used materials for buggy construction. The boxes for carriages and surreys are

21

The old-style mechanical brake has now been widely replaced by the hydraulic brake. The photo at right illustrates the most commonly used step for entering buggies.

now often made of molded fiber glass. Some seats for open buggies, shafts, and even wheels are now being made of this material.

The material for the gray and yellow top vehicles in Pennsylvania has traditionally been painted canvas duck. Some Amish still prefer this material but vinyl in the appropriate colors has become popular lately. The black material used by most plain people has been readily available over the years. The Wenger Mennonites in Pennsylvania have favored something called "Ford Truck Cushion Material" for their carriage tops.

How Long Does It Take to Build a Buggy?

It is hard to estimate how long it takes to construct a buggy from start to finish since it does not happen completely at one place. One Lancaster buggy maker estimated that 100 man hours went into a carriage but that did not include the construction of wheels nor tops which his shop has made elsewhere. That same shop produces about forty vehicles a year. A larger shop constructed seven vehicles in three weeks time. A Dover, Delaware man working by himself takes about one month to construct a buggy. He makes everything but the wheels.

There may be as many as eight coats of paint on the woodwork of a buggy. A mirror-like finish is achieved by sanding between each coat. Many Old Orders are not as particular as that, however, about the finish on their buggies.

How Long Does a Buggy Last?

Wheels are likely to need more repair than any other part of a buggy. Spokes may need to be replaced and the metal or rubber tires eventually wear out or get loose. The steel tires are shrunk by heating a section until it is red hot and then compressing it with a special device. The whole steel

Note the kerosene lantern on this Swiss-style Amish buggy from Adams County, Indiana. The battery-operated light (right) is standard on Lancaster buggies.

tire is then heated and put on the wooden wheel and cooled with water. Special bolts along the perimeter of the wheel hold the tire in place. Rubber tires require a special wheel with a channel and a machine to draw the rubber tight.

The long narrow wooden shafts connected to the axle and between which the horse stands are often broken and need to be repaired or replaced. The old style axles need periodic greasing and replacement of rattle-preventing leather washers. The new roller bearing axles do not need this maintenance but some say the metal on metal grinding makes more noise than the old style.

A buggy may receive a new paint job and a new top sometime during its life. Other than tightening bolts, a buggy does not need much other maintenance.

A typical Old Order may own no more than three passenger vehicles in his life. The first buggy he gets as a teenager serves until his early married years. As the family gets larger a roomier vehicle is acquired which may last until the children are grown and away from home, possibly a period of thirty or more years. At this time the older couple may go back to a smaller vehicle which will probably last the rest of their lives.

Do They Trade Them In?

Buggies are rarely traded in for newer models since styles change slowly or not at all. Older vehicles which are no longer suitable for Sunday use are kept around for odd errands and are used until they are not worth fixing. Older vehicles made of air dried wood seem to last much longer than those made of modern kiln dried wood.

Top: A close-up of an eliptic spring and a drop axle. Center: Note the fifth wheel turning device and the front spring. Bottom: Where the horse and buggy connect — the single tree attached to the harness traces.

	Two Seat Top Vehicle	One Seat Top Buggy	Open Buggy	Open Spring Wagon	Two Wheeled Cart
Lancaster, PA	$2,300	*	$1,400	$1,200	$ 450
Mifflin Co. PA (Renno)	1,750	*	1,200	1,400	600
New Wilmington, PA	1,050	$1,000	850	1,100	*
Holmes Co., Ohio (moderate)	1,800	1,600	*	1,100	450
Holmes Co., Ohio (conservative)	1,160	960	*	930	410
Geauga Co., Ohio	1,800	1,650	*	1,200	400
Somerset Co., PA	1,200	1,000	750	900	*
Dover, DE	1,700	1,500	*	900	500
Arthur, IL	2,975	2,450	1,150	1,350	575
Buchanan Co., IA	1,120	960	850	860	400
Adams Co., IN	*	*	800	900	350
Daviess Co., IN	*	*	775	875	325
La Grange Co., IN	1,550	1,450	*	1,300	550
Woolwich Mennonite	*	1,200	1,090	1,150	*
Venger Mennonite	1,700	1,650	*	1,200	500
Pike Mennonite	1,600	*	1,200	1,400	350

*Indicates vehicles that are not commonly used in the specified community.
The wide variety in price may partly be explained by differences in how elaborately the framework of the top is constructed, how fine the paint job is, and whether or not electric lights are present.

Restoration — A Big Business

A growing business for many Old Order buggy shops is the restoration of antique vehicles for collectors. Some shops do more of this kind of work than making plain buggies, and a few do only "fancy" restoration work. Some Old Orders are finding it profitable to take plain buggies which had been modified from fancy vehicles and changing them back to their original style.

An antique carriage auction is held three times a year at Paul Z. Martin Sales Stables near Intercourse, Pennsylvania. Here hundreds of buggies, carriages, and sleighs are sold to collectors and driving enthusiasts. These people, often wealthy New Englanders, have their own organizations, periodicals, and events. This new carriage trade relies heavily on the plain people for the restoration and upkeep of their vehicles and harnesses.

The plain buggy makers have a yearly reunion held at various locations across the United States and Canada. Here they can exchange ideas and hear of new developments in the buggy manufacturing business.

In the 1950's it was predicted that buggy production would necessarily end within one or two decades because of unavailability of parts. Somehow the business not only survived but is thriving.

4. Horses

It may come as a surprise to many people that very few plain people raise or train their own horses. Nearly all buggy horses are animals that were raised and trained for harness racing. Since only a small percentage of all horses that are intended for the races ever make the grade and those which are raced have a limited track life there is a rather large surplus of steeds. Individual Old Orders may go directly to the race track and buy a horse for their own use, but more commonly, "horse jockeys" will make the rounds to many race tracks and bring loads of driving horses back to the plain communities. These horses are either sold at special horse auctions like the ones at New Holland, Pennsylvania or Sugarcreek, Ohio, or sold directly to individual buyers by the horse dealer.

A driving horse may sell anywhere from $500 to $2200 depending on the quality of the animal. The price has gone up recently because much horse flesh is exported to Quebec and Europe for human consumption. Meat buyers are willing to pay four or five hundred dollars for an animal that could still be useful as a driving horse.

What Kind of Horses Are Used?

The breed of horse most often found among the plain people is the Standard Bred. This horse has been bred for endurance and speed and is well suited to pull a buggy. Standard Breds are most commonly of bay color and weigh between 900 and 1200 pounds. The American Saddle Horse or Saddle Bred can also make a good buggy horse. This breed is more elegant and slimmer than the Standard Bred. A few Morgans and crossbreds may also find their way to Old Order stables.

Driving horses are divided into two groups according to their gait: trotters and pacers. The trotter lifts his feet in alternate diagonal pairs; that is, the left front foot and the right hind foot are off the ground at the same time and so for the right front foot and left hind foot. A pacer which has a faster gait, raises both legs on the same side together. A Standard Bred may be a trotter or pacer or both. The Saddle Bred is only of the trotting variety.

What Do a Horse's Looks Tell You?

Of course an Old Order wants a good strong horse to pull his buggy. A certain amount can be told about a horse's disposition by examining its head. Ideally an even-tempered horse has uniform face lines, is broad between the eyes, long above the eyes, and wide between the base of the ears. A bulge below the eye line indicates wilfulness. Eyes set too far out and forward with furrows in the forehead show that the horse will be quick

Ideally an even-tempered horse has uniform face lines, is broad between the eyes, long above the eyes, and wide between the base of the ears. A bulge below the eye line indicates willfulness.

It may come as a surprise to many people that very few plain people raise or train their own horses.

to act and hard to restrain. A prominent forehead and dished face mean an ugly disposition including the tendency to kick and bite.

A fast horse is not always a safe horse. Many spirited animals are nervous and hard to control. One man, for example, had to take his horse up the road and back before he could load his family into the carriage after church. Some horses may balk, others shy from traffic. Large trucks are a terror to many horses and a frightened steed has more than once darted into the path of a speeding semi. Some people have been seriously injured or even killed by a kicking horse.

One horse went on a rampage after Sunday church services. The carriage trailing behind the frenzied animal banged into several vehicles as

Here an Amish farmer orchestrates his seven mule team. Mules and work horses are seldom used to pull buggies.

the horse raced past the long line of buggies leaving the meeting place. The children riding in the runaway carriage were terrified by the time the horse was brought under control.

When not in use a horse is kept in a stall in a barn or shed. Weather permitting, it may graze in a meadow. A well trained horse will come when called by its master.

A horse is usually fed twice a day. He receives hay and a special mixture of grains enriched with vitamins. Less food is given if the horse has

This winter scene, though modern, seems to be from another era. Sleighs are used less and less because roads are cleared so quickly.

been grazing. The stall receives a new bedding of straw every day. The old straw and manure are cleaned out once a week. A horse should be curried or brushed once a day and especially before being harnessed. A blanket is placed on the horse during cold weather when it is tied in the open or in a drafty stall. Special care is also taken not to overwork a horse in hot weather. It is given "wormer" three or four times a year to rid its system of internal parasites.

29

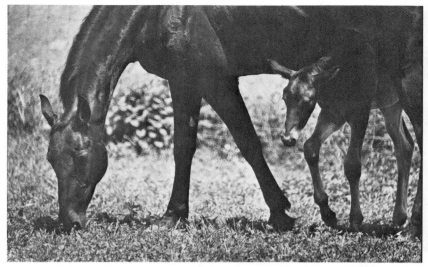

The average useful life of a horse is about fifteen years. The average speed of a horse is about eight to ten miles per hour. A good horse can travel about twenty miles without stopping.

Why Horseshoes?

A driving horse needs shoes to protect its feet on hard surfaced roads. These rims of iron are given an upturned toe pounded into the front edge and are shaped to the horse's foot. Nails are positioned so they protrude through the edge of the hoof. The points are clinched to hold the shoe on. Pads under the shoe may sometimes be necessary. Since the hooves grow like human nails the horseshoes need to be refitted or set periodically. The shoe is removed and the hoof is clipped and filed. The old shoe is put back on if it is still usable. Shoes need to be reset on the average of every ten weeks. Shoes are generally replaced every third time.

To give the shoe greater traction beads of borium or drill-tec are welded to the toe and heel. In Pennsylvania, borium, made of tungsten carbide particles, is used in summer, and drill-tec, made of ground-up drill bits, is used in winter. Some states outlaw drill-tec because of the damage it causes to roads.

One Old Order boy learned the hard way that horseshoes are quite necessary. One snowy morning after the rest of his family had gone to a church gathering the boy intended to come later with some food. Since the other horses were away he hitched the unshod farm horse to a sleigh. When only part way up a nearby hill the horse slipped and broke the shafts. The boy managed to get the sleigh and horse back home. He then hitched the horse to a carriage. At about the same spot the horse slipped again and broke the carriage shafts. The boy, the horse and the food went home and

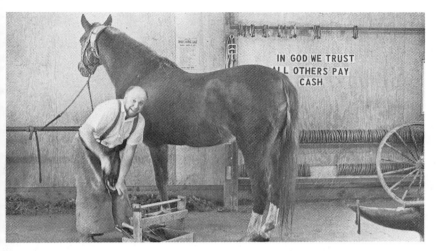

A driving horse needs shoes to protect its feet on hard surfaced roads. These rims of iron are given an upturned toe pounded into the front edge and are shaped to the horse's foot.

stayed there.

A person who shoes horses is technically a farrier (not a blacksmith, who is a worker in iron and might also shoe horses). Many Old Orders are full-time farriers or blacksmiths. In some small communities everyone shoes their own horses. In some larger settlements modern people fix up a truck with farrier equipment and go about to Old Order farms shoeing horses. A typical price would be $20 for resetting the shoes and $1 each for new shoes.

What About Endurance?

The average speed of a horse is about eight to ten miles an hour. Faster speeds are possible for short distances but racing is discouraged among Old Orders. A good horse can travel about twenty miles without stopping, but after that it must stop and rest for several hours. For longer trips, especially over hilly terrain, two horses are sometimes hitched to a carriage.

Each household head usually has only one driving horse. Young boys generally get a horse along with their first buggy. Large work horses and mules may also occupy the stable but these are rarely used for transportation.

The average useful life of a horse is about fifteen years (some may still be going strong in their twenties). When a horse ceases to be useful it often ends up at the sales ring and eventually becomes food for humans or animals.

5. Harness

A very important link between the horse and buggy is the harness. The harness not only attaches the horse to the buggy but is also the means by which the horse is guided. To the inexperienced eye the apparent tangle of leather straps may seem hopelessly complicated. A closer examination will find that each piece has a very definite purpose.

Two of the most important harness parts are the bit and reins. The bit is the metal piece that fits in the horse's mouth. The reins are long leather straps attached to the bit that extend to the driver. The reins are used to exert pressure on the bit in various ways, thus signalling the horse to perform different commands. An experienced driver can control a well-trained horse by holding both reins in one hand and rotating the hand to tighten one rein or the other. A high-strung horse requires both hands on the reins and constant pressure to hold the horse back.

A simple "giddap" or clicking with the tongue should suffice to get the horse moving. Slapping the reins is a frequent practice but is not recommended. A whip is sometimes used sparingly but it is the mark of a poor horseman to lash at the horse. A slight touch on the horse's shoulder should do.

In Lancaster County and some other Pennsylvania communities whips have never been allowed. In some places a simple stick serves to prod the horse.

A slacking up of the reins and speaking the horse's name is generally enough to accelerate the speed. To stop, the reins are pulled back sharply and the command, "whoa," is given.

It is very important for the harness to fit properly and to be in good condition. Periodic washing and oiling is essential to keep the leather pliable. Ordinarily a harness should need no repair for the first six years of its life. Points where leather and metal meet, such as the numerous buckles, tend to wear out first.

Most Old Order communities of any size have at least one harness shop. These shops often double as horse supply centers or shoe repair shops. Horse collars are generally the product of specialty shops. Many Old Order harness shops also cater to the non-plain trade.

In one Lancaster County shop a single harness with a collar costs $235. The collar alone brings $55. Harnesses made of nylon material are becoming popular in some areas. This material is less expensive than leather and does not require as much care.

An Amishman, above, prepares to hitch up his horse to his open buggy. The scene below pictures a Geauga County, Ohio hitching rail.

1. The **Bit** is the metal mouthpiece used to control the horse.
2. The **Reins** or **Lines** are attached to the bit, pass through a series of rings on the harness and extend to the driver of the vehicle.
3. The **Bridle** is the part of the harness that fits on the horse's head and holds the bit in place. **A halter** is similar but without a bit. It is used to tie or lead the horse when it is not in harness.
4. The **Blinders,** also called **winkers** or **blinkers,** are used to keep the horse from being frightened by objects behind and to the sides of it. Some very skittish horses are completely blindfolded.
5. The **Bearing reins** or **Check reins** are used to keep the horse's head up and in the right position. There are two main types: the over-check, going over the top of the horse's neck, and the side-check, going on each side of the neck. Both types attach to a hook on the saddle (9).
6. The **Collar** is the circular pad which fits around the horse's neck. The collar receives the pressure from the weight of the vehicle while it is being pulled.
7. The **Hames** are long metal pieces that fit snugly into the collar and to which the traces (8) are attached.
8. The **Traces** or **Tugs** are the part of the harness that actually attach the horse to the vehicle. They consist of heavy straps which are clipped to the hames (7) on one end and the single tree (23) on the other end.
9. The **Saddle** or **Gig Saddle** is positioned on the horse's back and has two turrets for the reins (2) to go through and a hook for the bearing rein (5).
10. The **Saddle Pad** is a protective pad under the saddle (9) often made of brightly colored sheep skin.

11. The **Girth** and **Bellyband** hold the saddle (9) in place. They are fastened around the horse's body.
12. The **Shaft Tugs** are sturdy leather rings through which the long wooden shafts (22) of the vehicle are placed.
13. The **Back band** attaches the shaft tugs (12) to the saddle (9) and girth (11).
14. The **Back strap** or **Turn back** extends from the saddle (9) across the horse's back to the crupper (15).
15. The **Crupper** is a sturdy leather loop at the end of the back strap (14) that fits under the horse's tail. These two items hold the saddle (9) in place.
16. The **Rings** and **Strap** slide through the back strap (14) and help hold the reins (2) in place.
17. The **Breeching** is a heavy strap which goes around the horse's rump (see 18).
18. The **Hold backs** or **Breeching Straps** are wrapped around the buggy shafts (22) and are snapped to the rings on each end of the breeching (17). These are not taken on and off with the rest of the harness. The breeching and hold backs serve to hold the vehicle away from the horse.
19. The **Hip straps** or **Loin straps** extend from the back strap (14) and serve to hold up the breeching (17).
20. The **Choke strap** attaches to the collar (6) and passes between the front legs to the bellyband (11). It is intended to hold down the collar (6).
21. The **Martingale** may take various forms but is usually a narrow Y-shaped strap attached either to the bridle (3), bit (1), or reins (2) on the forked end and the choke strap (20) on the other end. It is supposed to keep the horse's head down.

    The choke strap and martingale are common to Lancaster County Amish but few other groups use them.
22. The **Shafts** are the long narrow hickory pieces that extend from the buggy axle along each side of the horse. They serve to keep the horse in line with the vehicle.
23. The **Single Tree** or **Whiffle Tree** is mounted on the crosspiece of the shafts (22). The traces (8) are attached to each end of the single tree.
24. The **Tie rope** is used to tether the horse while parked. It may be kept in the vehicle or left on the horse's neck when not in use.

An alternate style of harness found in some communities features a breast strap or breast collar instead of the standard round collar. This consists of a wide band of leather which encircles the horse's chest. It is held in place by a neck strap. This is considered a more modern type of harness by many Old Orders.

For using two horses on a single vehicle a special set-up is required. The same basic harness is used but instead of the usual set of shafts a single "pole" or "tongue" extends from the vehicle axle between the two horses. The horse collars are attached to a neck yoke on the end of the pole.

6. Buggies and the Law

Many are the accounts of buggies being splintered by cars or trucks with the passengers killed or maimed. Various measures have been enacted by law to prevent motorists from slamming into these frail, slow-moving vehicles. Since the best way to protect buggies is to make them more obvious, a great deal of objection has been made by a people who wish to be unobtrusive.

Silver reflecting tape around the perimeter of a buggy was one of the first safety devices to be used, begun in Indiana in 1954. Later in the 50's battery operated red flasher lights were required. Some very conservative Amish objected to this flashy show. Twelve men were jailed in Hardin County, Ohio when they refused to comply with the law. For a brief period Indiana required buggies to display a red flag on a long pole.

The supposed ultimate in slow-moving vehicle (smv) protection was introduced in the 1960's in the form of large red-orange triangles. Indiana made the triangles compulsory for buggies in 1967. Ohio followed in 1974 and Pennsylvania in 1977. Again some of the most conservative Amish objected and several ended up in jail. In Hardin County, Ohio, buggies were confiscated and sold in order to pay for the fines. Eventually a compromise was made and the Hardin County Amish and Swartzentruber Amish in Ohio agreed to use silver reflecting tape. The "Nebraska Amish" of central Pennsylvania grudgingly agreed to use the triangles but a church rule dictates that they should be removed when the carriage is not in motion. Most Amish are more than glad for the protection the red triangles provide. David Wagler, the owner of an Amish book store in Ontario distributed brochures on the value of smv triangles in 1967.

Many Old Orders feel that triangles are as much a protection to the motorist as to the buggy driver. It is also felt that it is a privilege to be allowed on the roads with automobiles and every effort should be made to comply with laws and safety requirements for horse-drawn vehicles.

Smooth black-topped highways are welcomed by car and buggy drivers alike but the wear caused by horseshoes and steel tires has caused a problem for both. The Amish in Indiana willingly agreed to make use of less abrasive metal on their horseshoes.

Indiana has required license plates for horse-drawn vehicles since 1954. So far it is the only state to do so. The Geauga County, Ohio Amish may buy a vehicle identification plate voluntarily from the county government. This is a service offered in order to identify accident victims.

In many Amish communities, signs warn motorists in words or symbols that they are approaching a horse-drawn vehicle area.

Individual states take it upon themselves to warn motorists of horse-drawn vehicles. Top left, Pennsylvania; top middle, Delaware; top right, Ohio; center left, New York; center right, Kansas. Despite many precautions accidents do occasionally happen.

7. Harassment

Some motorists become annoyed at buggy traffic and vent their frustrations by honking their horns and cutting in dangerously close when they finally have the opportunity to pass.

Of a more serious nature are the malicious acts of vandalism and cruel pranks played on the Old Order people. Some young delinquents have made a sport of bumping carriages with their cars or jumping on the backs of buggies and grabbing the drivers' hats. Some hoodlums have tried to stop and rob buggies by blocking the roads with their cars. Others have jumped out at buggies at night and grabbed the horse's reins in an effort to stop them. Most of these thugs find it rather difficult to stop a horse. Some that have been successful have threatened buggy drivers with baseball bats. One Amish boy who was stopped by some roughnecks shouted to his horse, "Kick 'em!" The assailants fled in terror even though the horse had no idea what the command meant.

There have been cases of buggies being stolen and burned or dragged behind a car until demolished. One horse was shot in the neck while travelling down the road. A seventeen year-old boy from La Grange County, Indiana was killed when a large piece of asphalt was hurled through the front of his buggy by someone in a passing car. Similarly a baby was killed in Adams County, Indiana when several youths in a pickup truck pelted an Amish open buggy with stones and pieces of drainage tile. In this community many local boys made a sport of throwing objects at Amish people and houses. This did not come to the light of the law until recently because the Amish did not believe in reporting the incidents.

Persons who ride in buggies are vulnerable. Some suffer harassment. On the whole however, such incidents are not common.

The defenseless, serving attitude of Old Order communities can make them appear easy victims. But the strength of Christian community prevails. These people believe that love overcomes evil. Even curiosity about these people may become a form of harassment.

8. Alternate Transportation

Contrary to some fictional accounts there are very few Amish or other Old Order people who have never ridden in a motor vehicle. Practically all Old Order groups allow their members to make use of trains, buses, taxis, and other hired vehicles. Actual driving of motor vehicles is universally forbidden, and indiscreet and unnecessary hiring of taxis is warned against. A **Family Life** article admonishes against hiring a driver with a motor home for long family excursions. Another article shows the inconsistency of some who hire a driver to take them to a distant grocery store in order to get green stamps.

In most Old Order communities there are usually one or more outsiders who make their living by providing a taxi service for the plain people. A controversy developed in Lancaster in 1977 over the Amish taxi drivers who had not secured the proper licenses from the Public Utilities Commission. Despite organized protest forty-one drivers were compelled to secure licenses.

Youth Might Own Cars

It is a well-known fact that in the larger settlements many unbaptized Old Order youth own cars. In the more conservative communities they do so on the sly. In the more liberal communities these wayward youth may provide convenient transportation for the rest of the family. The writer has even seen one Amish father helping his non-member son do mechanical work on his car. Another Amish man from Ohio took a "pre-honeymoon" to Niagara Falls with his future wife before he was baptized and married and had to put away his car. This man no longer belongs to the Old Order Amish and such conduct is frowned upon by the Old Order churches. Many of the more recently established communities maintain a stricter control on car usage by youths.

Tractor Travel

Among a few Old Order groups modern tractors with pneumatic tires are often used as transportation. In some communities passenger trailers especially designed to accommodate the whole family are hitched to tractors. In these communities buggies are seldom used except on Sunday. Most Old Order groups feel that this kind of tractor use is only a step away from using cars. In order to restrict tractor travel many Old Orders forbid pneumatic tires or limit the use of tractors to belt power

The striking contrast shown above illustrates how the Old Order have become a peculiarity in the modern world. Air travel is either severely limited or strictly forbidden by most Old Orders. Bicycles are allowed by many Old Order groups as shown by these parked by a Wenger Mennonite meetinghouse in Lancaster County, Pa. (below).

A few Old Order groups, like the King Amish of Hartville, Ohio (top), make extensive use of pneumatic tire tractors, even using them for shopping trips and visiting. Many Old Orders require that tractors have steel tires so they are not used for transportation. Another way of limiting mobility among most Lancaster Amish is by allowing scooters (bottom left) but forbidding bicycles. Only rarely will one see a plain person riding horseback (bottom right).

only. Among some Amish groups, tract⌐ s which are used for belt power, must be pulled to their working location by horses.

Some Old Orders make extensive use of bicycles, notably the Old Order Mennonites of Pennsylvania and the Amish of Holmes County, Ohio and Elkhart and La Grange Counties, Indiana. In Lancaster County the majority of Amish forbid bicycles. The restriction on bicycles is an effort to restrict mobility.

Horseback riding is extremely rare among Old Order people. One will occasionally see a child riding a pony or a young man out for a ride but almost never would a person ride a horse to church. Obviously the problem of modesty is involved for women and, of course, only one or two people can conveniently ride a horse with room for very little baggage.

The Amish community at Sarasota, Florida, although recognized as Old Order, does not have a single horse and buggy. The inhabitants are mostly retirees and seasonal visitors who make extensive use of bicycles and adult tricycles.

In Geauga County, Ohio where many Amish work in factories, an entire church district may occupy a very small thickly settled area. In this case most people would walk to church and work and have very little need for horses and buggies.

Air Travel

Since air travel is about as contrary to the Old Order lifestyle as anything can be, this form of transportation is either strongly discouraged or absolutely forbidden. In Lancaster County air travel is allowed for emergency situations only. One case involved an expectant mother who had to be rushed to a hospital during a snow storm via helicopter. Some communities allow air travel over the ocean but not for intracontinental jaunts. Other groups restrict air travel for immigration purposes only. One group excommunicated a number of people who migrated to Paraguay by air.

Historically the plain people have discouraged jobs involved with stage coaches, trains, or ships, no doubt because these occupations would keep one away from home for long periods of time. There have been few restrictions on using these forms of transportation however.

9. What Are the Main Buggy Styles?

The types and styles of vehicles used by the plain people are very much subject to local custom and church regulations. In most older communities one will find a standarization of vehicles. Distinctive features have developed over the years in each community and group. Variation due to personal preference is at a minimum. Thus all Lancaster Amish carriages have gray tops, straight sides and rounded roof corners and all Holmes County Amish buggies have black tops, angled-in sides, and square roof corners. One would never see a Lancaster carriage in Holmes County or vice versa.

Buggies in New Settlements

When people from several different older communities come together to form a new settlement a variety of different vehicles may be seen for a while in the same area. Eventually, as new buggies are needed, a composite style develops.

In some cases people moving into a new community must modify their buggies to conform to church regulations. For example, one family had to decrease the size of their buggy windows by painting in all but the required opening in the glass.

Sometimes new communities are formed by people of all the same background. When this happens the original vehicle style remains unchanged. Thus, Lancaster style carriages have spread over a wide area of central Pennsylvania.

Vehicle terminology varies from one area to the next. In several communities like Arthur, Illinois, New Wilmington, Pennsylvania, and Dover, Delaware, all passenger vehicles are called buggies; only utility vehicles have a different name. From this generic sense of the word comes the title of this book.

Buggies Have Many Names

In many communities various types of vehicles have different designations. In Lancaster County the standard two seat vehicle is called a carriage and the open one seat variety is called a buggy. In most of the mid-western communities a single seat enclosed vehicle is called a buggy or top buggy and a two seat vehicle is called a surrey. Among the more conservative mid-western groups a simpler style of two seat vehicle is

Amish Vehicles	Total Number of Districts	Style Variations in Use	Districts using Described Style
ennsylvania Styles	122	(C) white, brown, black	8
		(B) yellow, brown	1
		(B) dark yellow, black	12
		(A, B) yellow, black	1
		(A, B) black	11
		(A) gray, black	89
hio Styles	310	All are black	
		(E) small dash	59
		(all with steel tires)	
		(no windows — 42)	
		(with windows — 17)	
		(D) wide dash with roll curtains	161
		(all with windows and steel tires)	
		(no storm front — 56)	
		(with storm front — 105)	
		(D) wide dash with sliding doors	90
		(all with windows and storm fronts)	
		(steel tires — 47)	
		(rubber tires — 43)	
diana	99	All are black with windows, wide dash, and storm front	
		roll curtains, steel tires	64
		sliding doors, steel tires	9
		sliding doors, rubber tires	26
icts in which both Ohio and Indiana Styles are used			10
wiss	42	All are black	
		No back rest	30
		With back rest	12

Vehicles of Other Groups	Number of Churches		
ennonite	69	(Style variation numbers also refer to Amish section)	
		(M, K) Pike (no windows)	12
		(M, K) Hoover	3
		(M, N) Wenger	31
		(K, L, M) Ontario	15
		(O, H) Indiana	3
		(N, H) Virginia	5
erman Baptist	6	(M, H)	
iver Brethren	2	(M)	

le K is used as an alternate vehicle in a number of communities. The surrey and top wagon type, -seat vehicles, (not shown) are used in the Ohio and Indiana style areas. Communities might use : or the other of these types and sometimes both.

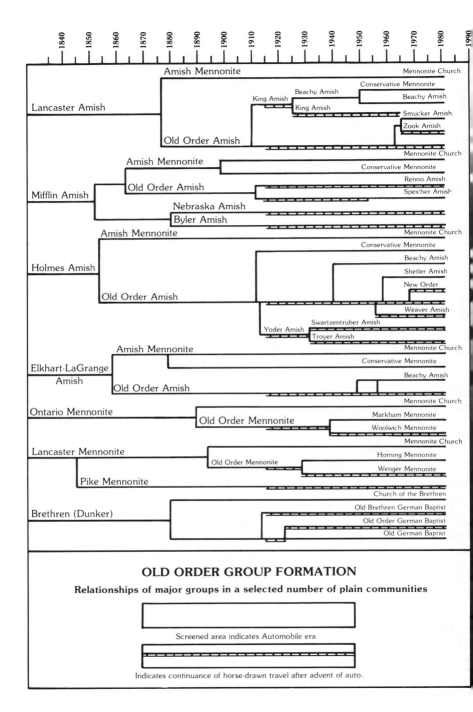

OLD ORDER GROUP FORMATION

Relationships of major groups in a selected number of plain communities

Screened area indicates Automobile era

Indicates continuance of horse-drawn travel after advent of auto.

referred to as a spring wagon or top wagon. The latter term is preferred by this author to avoid confusion with the open utility vehicle.

The open spring wagon, the utility vehicle with one seat and a hauling space in back, has a wide variety of local names. In Holmes County, Ohio it is a "Hack"; in Arthur, Illinois a "Buckboard"; in Dover, Delaware, a "Durban"; in Adams County, Indiana, a "Johnny wagon"; in Daviess County, Indiana, a "Long John"; and in Aylmer, Ontario, a "Democrat."

A recent style of spring wagon, featuring an open bed or long storage compartment in back and an enclosed driver's seat will be referred to as a "cab wagon" in this book. In Pennsylvania a carriage-like vehicle with heavier suspension on the rear axle is called a market wagon or peddle wagon.

A number of vehicles used by the plain people are somewhat out of the scope of this book. These include heavy farm wagons and other agricultural vehicles. The special wagons designed to transport benches from one Amish meetingplace to the next are found in each Amish church district. In Lancaster County the Old Order Amish and Mennonites make use of specially designed hearses. In Holmes County vehicles resembling a cab wagon transport the coffins.

Sleighs, cutters, and bobsleds are rarely used in most communities and are not of any special style. Few new snow vehicles are produced. Enough antique vehicles are around to serve the limited demand.

Four Main Styles

Horse-drawn vehicles among the plain people may be divided into four general styles based upon the basic shape of the body. The names for these styles are based upon the state or group in which they predominate.

    I. Pennsylvania Style. Straight sides. The standard vehicle has two seats with entrance ways to the front seat only. The tops may be black, gray, white, or several shades of yellow.

    II. Ohio Style. Angled-in sides. The standard vehicle has one seat. The tops are black only.

    III. Indiana Style. The top is built around the base of the seat backrest. The standard vehicle has one seat. The tops are black only.

    IV. Swiss Style. Vehicles with no tops in communities where tops are not allowed. Black only.

The Old Order Mennonites, Brethren groups, and Old Colony Mennonites will be treated separately since their vehicles may encompass more than one of the basic styles.

Within a given style there are a wide variety of sub-styles. Windows, dashboards, roll-up side and back curtains, sliding doors, hinged doors, battery operated lights, kerosene or gas lanterns, storm fronts (windshields), sun visors, running gear, steel stires, and rubber tires, are some details which vary from one community to the next.

Size of circles indicates approximate population of the various communities. Names in all capital letters are county names; others are names of towns.

10. Pennsylvania

The Pennsylvania style Amish buggy has straight sides and comes in yellow, white, black or gray. The gray Lancaster vehicle, above, is the most common.

Pennsylvania style vehicles bear a strong resemblance to a number of common 19th century American vehicles with stationary tops and straight sides. One of the oldest types was known as a Dearborn wagon which originated early in the century. Other vehicles which are similar if not identical were the Depot wagon and Carryall. The names Jersey wagon, Germantown wagon, and Rockaway might also be applied to similar vehicles but these terms were generally reserved for more elaborate conveyances.

This type of vehicle no doubt appealed to the plain people because it could double as a utility vehicle and was not considered a pleasure carriage.

The Lancaster Gray Carriage

Since Lancaster County, Pennsylvania receives more tourists than any other Amish community the vehicles of these folk are by far the most well-known. Actually only about 15% of all Old Order Amish use the familiar gray-topped carriage. In many ways the Lancaster Amish are quite different from their brethren farther west. In some ways they have kept old customs that the majority of Amish have abandoned; in other ways they have accepted innovations which other Amish shun. This applies in matters of dress, technology and buggies.

In 1869 Phebe Earle Gibbons described Lancaster Amish vehicles as being covered with yellow oilcloth. Deacon Benjamin Hoover (b. 1874) of the Old Order Mennonites stated that Amish vehicles seen in his boyhood were about half yellow and half gray. In 1911 a writer states, "The yellow of the oilcloth has disappeared, lead color having taken its place, and any style of wagon is orthodox. A careful observer has said that where Amish conveyances are brought together at services or funerals scarcely any two are alike." (**The Pennsylvania German,** June 1911 p. 337).

Gibbons also spoke of the introduction of steel eliptic springs among the Amish. Apparently they were common when she wrote in 1869 but she told of an infirm Amishman of an earlier time who secretly had springs placed beneath his carriage seat ("Pennsylvania Dutch and Other Essays," 1882).

Originally Lancaster carriages had roll curtains at the front entrance ways and no dashboard. As the auto age progressed and increased visibility became imperative the side curtains were used less and less. Today these items are very seldom seen in Lancaster County. A canvas apron snapped to the carriage box and side posts and drawn up to the driver's chin gives some weather protection in open front vehicles.

A Buggy "Station Wagon"

A heavier type vehicle with extra suspension on the rear axle is called a market wagon in Lancaster County. It was formerly a common practice to take produce to city markets in such wagons. Although this activity has ceased, the market wagon has survived. This market wagon might be compared with an automobile station wagon. The end tailgate drops down and the back panel lifts up to facilitate loading and unloading. Like a station wagon the market wagon can be used with or without a back seat.

The Lancaster market wagon (left and far right above) has an enclosed front, a removable second seat, and back panel which opens. The old style carriage, center, has an open front (newer ones are enclosed).

Calling the open buggy "the courting buggy" is incorrect. Increasingly young people are using the top carriage, and the open buggy is often driven by older adults.

Market wagons usually came equipped with a sun visor and a closed-in front featuring sliding doors with large glass windows and a storm front, a windshield dashboard combination. For some reason these features were not allowed on the regular carriage. Perhaps this was because the first market wagons used by the Amish were second-hand delivery vehicles produced by non-plain people and it was considered too much bother to alter them to Amish standards.

Beginning in the late 1920's a few Lancaster Amish began putting sliding doors and storm fronts on regular carriages. This was strongly discouraged at first and the practice did not increase until the 1950's and was officially tolerated about 1960 except in the conservative southern districts. Early storm fronts had a fabric panel below the windshield and the whole front could be snapped on and off.

Currently ministers may use market wagons with closed fronts during the week and occasionally on Sunday, but they may not use the new closed front carriage. When a man is ordained the permanent storm front on his carriage is to be removed, but the sliding doors are often left on.

New style closed front carriages are still discouraged in the southern part of the main settlement and the Lancaster daughter communities at Mechanicsville, Maryland, Loganton, Pennsylvania, and Danville, Pennsylvania.

The characteristic features of a carriage and market wagon have been very much mixed in Lancaster County. The only remaining differences are that a market wagon is a little larger, has extra suspension on the rear axle, and a tail gate that drops down. An increasingly common style of carriage called a "combination" has a lift-up back panel but only one spring on the back.

Open Buggies Disappearing

With the widespread acceptance of closed front carriages came the large scale abandonment of the traditional open buggy (often offensively called a "courting buggy" by outsiders) by Lancaster Amish youth. One still sees these lightweight rigs driven by young and old but few new open buggies are being built. In the conservative southern districts and in some daughter colonies open buggies are more common.

A distinctive feature of Lancaster open buggies is the absence of a dashboard. This is a custom found in no other community except those related to Lancaster. A protective fabric apron called a mud-splasher hanging from the shaves and axle serves the same purpose as a dash. These are also used on other vehicles.

Two-wheeled carts are fairly new to the Lancaster area but are becoming increasingly common. Cab wagons of mid-western origin are becoming popular although they are still far out-numbered by the traditional open spring wagon.

Traditionally the spring wagon, left, provided no shield from the elements. A new vehicle for hauling purposes becoming more common in Lancaster is the cab wagon, right.

Electric Lights Accepted

Electric lights on carriages have been accepted by Lancaster Amish since the 1920's. Before this time they were a controversial matter. One Amish man was repeatedly admonished to get rid of his battery operated carriage lights. He finally promised to have no more to do with these contrivances. This man held true to his word even after nearly every Amish family in the County had electric lights on their vehicles.

Headlights with high and low beams and combination flasher lights and turn signals are standard equipment on Lancaster vehicles. At least two red reflectors are placed on the back of a carriage; young people may use many more. Luminous tape is often a source of decoration.

Lancaster Amish have never allowed whips or whip sockets on their vehicles in contrast to many other Amish, even the most conservative midwestern groups.

Lancaster style gray top vehicles have been dispersed to other parts of the state with the formation of over a dozen daughter colonies. These include the Pennsylvania settlements at Myerstown, Littlestown, Rebersburg (Brush Valley), Loganton (Sugar Valley), Mill Hall (Nittany Valley), Newburg (Cumberland Valley), Danville (Susquehanna Valley), Loysville, Delta, Trout Run, Elizabethville, White Deer, and Dry Run.

The New Order Amish in Lancaster County and Mifflinburg, Pennsylvania have Lancaster style vehicles but allow rubber tires. They also allow more modern farm machinery than do the Old Orders.

The oldest and largest Lancaster based settlement is at Mechanicsville, Maryland. Here many people have a very long gray top wagon with facing side seats in the back.

Mifflin County

The Kishacoquillas Valley in Mifflin County, Pennsylvania was first settled by Amish in 1791. This community has been known for its conservatism and also for its fragmentation. Perhaps the greatest variety in horse-drawn vehicles in a single area can be found in this community. There are five distinct groups of Old Order Amish in the Valley at present. The two most conservative groups have white-topped vehicles, another has yellow tops and two others use black tops.

Nebraska Amish Buggies Plainer

The Nebraska Amish originated in Mifflin County but have daughter colonies at Woodward, McClure, and Winfield in Pennsylvania. They received their name from a bishop from Nebraska who helped them organize in 1881. There are presently three distinct groups of these people but all have similar customs.

The Nebraska Amish are considered to be the most conservative of all Amish. Their dress, homes, and vehicles reflect customs that were prevalent among the Amish a century or more ago but have now been modified in other groups.

Among the Nebraskans there seems to be a preference for brown and white. The men typically wear brown trousers and white shirts and their carriages have brown boxes and white tops. The running gear on the Nebraska vehicles is black however. Carriages have four supporting posts on each side rather than the usual three. There are usually two sets of roll

White and brown are the colors distinguishing the vehicles of the most conservative of all Amish groups, the Nebraska Amish of central Pennsylvania.

up curtains on each side although some individuals leave off the front curtains. The curtains on the most conservative Nebraska carriages have fasteners using leather tabs and metal rings. Metal twist fasteners are now being used on some vehicles. There are no windows, storm fronts, or dashes on Nebraska vehicles. The simple front seat has a back that folds down to allow entry to the back seat. The seats are unupholstered but are usually covered with a blanket.

The two eliptic springs are attached directly to the box rather than to a spring bar. The shafts are nearly straight having only a slight curve at the very end.

The step plates are mounted at the cross piece on the shafts rather than on the box. This makes it necessary to enter from the front rather than the side. This was a feature that carriages of other Pennsylvania plain people had early in this century. This includes the Lancaster Amish, Pike Mennonites, and Old Order River Brethren. Long-bodied market wagon type vehicles are found among the Nebraska Amish. These are equipped with three eliptic springs and may be used as a three seat vehicle as well as for utility purposes. Open spring wagons are painted brown. They have simple back rests and may be equipped with side boards. The Nebraska Amish do not use single seat open buggies. Kerosene lanterns are the only approved lighting devices.

Byler Amish Drive Yellow Tops

The Byler Amish divided with the Nebraska Amish in 1881, and both groups originate from an 1849 break with the larger Amish group in Mifflin County. Although limited to only one district around Belleville and having only about 90 members the Byler Amish are widely known for their distinctive bright yellow carriage tops. The origin of this custom is vague. One Amishman thought that the white paint on early carriages turned yellow and eventually people just started painting the tops yellow. Another explanation is that tops were originally made of unbleached linen which would have been a pale yellow. The writer's theory is that the Amish made use of the same type of oilcloth that had been traditionally used for rain coats or "slickers." The custom is very old and is certainly not an effort to be more visible on the highways as a measure of safety. Today a vinyl material for the yellow tops has replaced the painted duck formerly used. This material is brighter in color but has produced more uniformity in hue on Byler carriages than was possible with paint.

The most common type of Byler vehicle resembles a Lancaster County market wagon only with a yellow top. These vehicles have black boxes and running gear, rounded roof corners, storm fronts, sliding doors with large windows, sun visors, three eliptic springs, a lift-up back door,

The Byler Amish, also of central Pennsylvania, use yellow and black vehicles. Note the square corners. Note also the sliding doors on the carriage, right.

and a roll-up back curtain. They may or may not have a back window. This type of wagon is perhaps more often used as a family vehicle rather than for utility purposes.

These people also use a second vehicle as a true market wagon. These wagons have long bodies and tops made of plywood or masonite. The black box extends about halfway up the sides and the sliding or hinged doors are either yellow or black. The back door also may be hinged from the side. These vehicles are often a paler yellow than the other types. One example had a partition with a window between the driver's seat and the rear compartment. Square corners and a roof overhanging in the front to form a sort of visor are typical features.

Two-seated carriages with square corners are an older type vehicle among the Byler group. In recent years storm fronts and sliding doors have been allowed on this type carriage. As in Lancaster County such closed in carriages have largely replaced the open buggy among the young people.

Open spring wagons are still quite common to the Byler group.

The Renno Black Box

The Renno Amish of Mifflin County are the largest Old Order group in the Valley. They currently have five districts. They have received the nickname "one suspender Amish" from the men's curious practice of using only one strap to hold up their pants. This is also a custom among the Byler Amish.

The Renno vehicles are all black. The standard carriage has two seats with a folding front seat. The side and back curtains are rolled up and an additional short curtain is used in the front as a bit of additional weather protection. There are no windows or storm fronts. The box extends rather

Renno vehicles are black. Note the roll curtains and the single headlight. Th carriages do not have windows, as illustrated by the Renno-style carriage from County, left.

high in the back but is cut out at the doorways. Only one headlight is used by the Rennos.

The Renno market or top wagons have rounded roofs and are equipped with storm fronts and sliding doors. As with Lancaster market wagons these vehicles have a removable back seat. There are generally no back windows in Renno market wagons and the back curtain rolls up as well as lifts up. Some vehicles are similar to a Lancaster County "combination."

These closed front vehicles are a fairly recent innovation among the Rennos and have not gained full approval. At present they are not to be driven to Sunday church services.

A few long square cornered black market wagons like those described for the Bylers are found among the Rennos. Open buggies are commonly used by the Rennos but unlike Lancaster buggies they have dashes and narrow back rests. Open spring wagons frequently have blue or green side boards thus adding to the colorful array in Mifflin County.

The Amish community in Juniata County was started in 1950 by Renno Amish and Amish from Holmes and Wayne Counties, Ohio. The Juniata people use vehicles which are nearly identical to Renno types. Small Renno settlements are also located at Mercersburg, Pennsylvania and Newport, New York.

The very small "New Order" Amish group in Mifflin County was comprised of both Byler and Renno elements; hence both yellow and black vehicles could be found among them. Today the shift to all black vehicles has been nearly completed. Most New Order carriages have sliding doors, rubber tires, and mud splashers, but otherwise look like Renno carriages.

New Wilmington Variety

The Amish first settled in northern Lawrence County around New Wilmington, Pennsylvania, in 1847. These people came from Mifflin County and have always had a close relationship with the Byler group in that community. Most of the vehicles of the New Wilmington Amish have dark yellow-brown tops. This color approaches the color commonly seen

The open buggy from New Wilmington features the narrow backrest but includes a dash. The buggy from this community has a dark yellow top and roll curtains.

on circus tents and perhaps the Amish obtained this same type of canvas for their tops many years ago. The box and running gear on all vehicles are black. The new Wilmington carriages are the same basic shape as those of the Renno and Byler groups. Small windows in the rear curtain and side roll curtains and a detachable single pane storm front used in cold weather have been used since the 1930's. One battery operated headlight gained acceptance in the 1920's and flasher lights are standard.

Open buggies with dashboards and narrow rod supported backrests are quite common. However since the 1940's many young people own single seat top buggies, something almost unknown in other communities discussed in this section. A boy's buggy has the back curtain tacked down until after he is married. After that it is taken loose and fixed with snaps so it can be rolled up. A seat is then provided for small children in the narrow rear compartment. When the family gets larger a carriage with two full seats is obtained.

The New Wilmington version of the market wagon is similar to the longer variety of Byler & Renno market wagons and is called a "peddle wagon." These vehicles, unlike others used in this area, have white plywood tops and black sliding doors, boxes, and running gear. These wagons are never equipped with back seats. In addition to typical open spring wagons a special type of wagon with a very high seat is seen in New Wilmington. Its design allows a few more milk cans to be placed under the seat. New Wilmington style buggies are also found at Mayville, New York and Lander, Pennsylvania.

Enon Valley Details

The Amish community at Enon Valley, Pennsylvania, was started by

Two unusual vehicles found in the New Wilmington area are the high-seat spring wagon, designed to carry milk cans, and the peddle wagon which has a white top and sliding doors.

New Wilmington people in 1924. Some Nebraska Amish also moved to this location. The carriages here are very similar to those of the mother settlement except that they usually have brown boxes and running gear and the tops are brighter yellow. Electric headlights are not seen; however side-mounted blinkers are used. Detachable storm fronts are acceptable. Black open buggies are commonly used by the young people.

The settlement at Turbotville, Pennsylvania, is made up mostly of former Enon Valley residents. A switch to all black buggies was made here. There is also a trend toward using sliding doors and rubber tires.

11. Ohio

Ohio has a larger Old Order Amish population than any other state. In 1981 there were twenty communities and 173 church districts in the "Buckeye" state. The two largest settlements centering in Holmes County and Geauga County account for three-fourths of the Amish in Ohio and rank first and fourth in size for all Amish communities.

The same general style of buggy is used throughout all Ohio. (Two exceptions would be Hicksville, Ohio and Belle Center, Ohio where Indiana style buggies also appear.) Some buggies are extremely simple while others have all the extras. Tradition has it that Ohio Amish used only open buggies and wagons until the early 1900's. At this time some people began making stationary tops for their vehicles. The pattern chosen involved a framework over the entire buggy body with sides angling in from the edge of the seat to the buggy box. A popular American buggy called a Jenny Lind was very similar and may have been the basis for the idea. The small dash remained unchanged on early Ohio buggies. Tops were also put on long bodied spring wagons. These could be used with or without a back seat.

In Holmes, Wayne, Tuscarawas, and Coshocton Counties in Ohio there are 102 contiguous Amish districts, which includes eight distinct groups. The largest group has fifty-seven districts and is pretty much in the middle of the liberal-conservative spectrum. We will refer to these as the moderates. Locally they are called the Old Orders while other groups

The Ohio style buggy is the most popular among the Amish of North America. It features angled-in sides and is always black. The one pictured above is a simpler version from Holmes County.

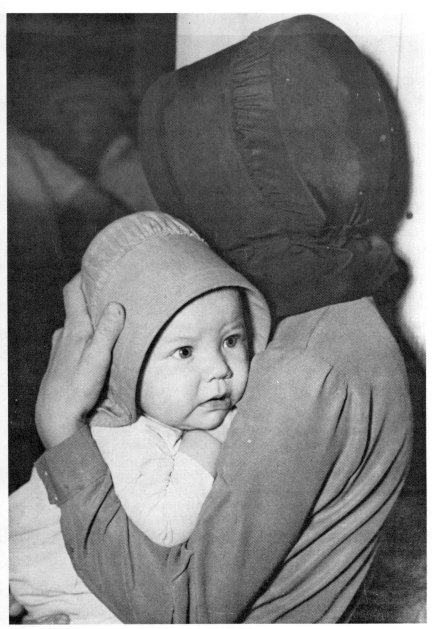

Children are treasured in the Old Order communities. While Amish society may appear austere to outsiders, many of the children feel tenderness and choose to stay. It is conscious decisions, such as retaining the buggy, which hold the communities together. Amish population has doubled over the past two decades.

The open spring wagon, top left, is called a "hack" in Ohio. The cab-style wagon above is called a "top hack." Two-wheeled carts are also quite common among Holmes County groups.

generally carry the name of the founding bishop.

Buggy Changes Among "Moderate" Groups

The vehicles of the Holmes County moderates have undergone various changes in the last fifty years. Beginning in the early 1930's the surrey type two seat vehicle began appearing in Holmes County. Battery operated buggy lights first made their appearance on the buggies of Holmes County young people in the mid 1930's. At this time the young folks had only open buggies. In the late 1930's a trend was set when two sons of an Amish bishop began using top buggies with wide dashes. In little over a decade the wide dash became standard on Holmes County vehicles.

In the early 1940's someone got the idea to put a permanent panel of top fabric down the side of a surrey parallel with the front seat. In this way the two sets of roll curtains would not have to be as clumsily wide. This feature eventually became universally accepted among Holmes County moderates and the surrey completely replaced the top wagon.

The open spring wagon is called a hack in Holmes County. A variation which this writer calls a cabwagon is referred to as top hack. This Amish style pickup truck which came into general use in the 1950's is probably descended from the mid-western style hearse which is very similar in appearance.

Storm fronts, the buggy windshield, are a fairly recent innovation in Holmes County. Several districts in the moderate group around New Bedford still discourage their use. Windows in the side panels are also very recent innovations and many buggies do not have them. Ornamental panels with cutout designs along the edge appear frequently on the top front border of Holmes County buggies.

Open buggies are very rare among Holmes County moderates but two wheeled carts are very common. These lightweight vehicles are especially suited to traverse the very hilly terrain in this part of Ohio. Some carts are even equipped with electric lights. The small Dan Miller group have vehicles like those of the moderate group although some use rubber tires.

Geauga Varieties

The buggies used in the forty Amish districts centered in Geauga County, Ohio are very similar to those of Holmes County. One almost undiscernable difference is the slight outward projection of the roofs on Geauga buggies.

Two unique innovations in Geauga are the flare board, a slanting piece of wood at the top edge of the dash to deflect stones kicked up by the horse, and the wear bar, a bent metal rod used to prevent wear by the reins on the dash or flare board. Like the Holmes County moderates Geauga buggies have roll-up side curtains. Windows in the side panels have been standard in Geauga for many years.

A predominate style of two seat vehicle has not been established in Geauga. Top wagons in longer and shorter versions and surreys with and without divider panels can all be seen. Some surreys and top wagons have two facing side seats in the back and a step to enter from the rear.

Storm Fronts Out for Conservative Groups

Ten districts in Geauga County do not permit storm fronts. Six of these districts form a separate conservative group. Geauga daughter colonies at Smicksburg, Pennsylvania, Troutville, Pennsylvania, Lore City, Ohio, and Dunnville, Kentucky, have the simple style of Geauga buggy without storm front or flare board. These extras are allowed in other Geauga related settlements at Spartansburg, Pennsylvania, Clymer, New York, and Guysmills, Pennsylvania.

Thirteen districts in the Holmes-Wayne County community referred to as the Andy Weaver group are similar to the conservative minority in Geauga County. Storm fronts are not allowed by these people. Surreys with divider panels are common among the Weaver people. A related group at Lakeville, Ohio, have some surreys without the divider panels and unlike the Weavers discourage the use of battery buggy lights.

The Hostetler Amish in Holmes and Wayne Counties and the Danville, Ohio settlement have buggy regulations like those of the Weaver group.

In the 1950's a number of conservative minded people decided to move out of Holmes and Wayne Counties. A new settlement was started near Ashland, Ohio. These Amish have retained the old style narrow dash and use only kerosene buggy lanterns. Instead of the usual red triangles the Ashland folk make their own triangles of gray reflector tape with a round red reflector in the middle. Top wagons with and without divider panels predominate in the Ashland settlement but surreys are also

All of these vehicles originate from Geauga County, Ohio: upper left, a typical Geauga-style buggy from Spartansburg, Pa.; lower left, a simpler version from Jackson Center, Pa. (note the oval window); top right, a Geauga top wagon; bottom right, a surrey.

present. The Fredericktown, Ohio Amish have vehicles like those of Ashland.

Conservative Amish from LaGrange County, Indiana began moving into Hardin County, Ohio in the 1950's. The Ohio style buggy replaced the newcomers' Indiana style and the small dash became their standard. Top wagons without side panels became the accepted two seat vehicle. The back roll curtains in Hardin County extend the whole width of the back and conform to the shape of the vehicle. Kerosene lanterns are the only lights on Hardin County buggies and slow moving vehicle triangles are not allowed.

Groups similar to the Hardin County Amish exist at Paoli, Indiana, Becks Mills, Ohio, Marrietta, Ohio, and Chesterhill, Ohio.

The settlement at Atlantic, Pennsylvania was begun by Geauga County, Ohio Amish in 1924. A daughter settlement from Atlantic was begun at Jackson Center, Pennsylvania in 1942. Both of these settlements have kept the small dash and the older style top wagons and surreys without divider panels. No windows appear on the side panels or roll curtains. Battery operated lights are allowed.

About 1913 an ultra-conservative group led by Bishop Sam Yoder broke away from the majority group in Holmes County, Ohio. The group later became identified by the name of its second bishop, Jacob Swartzentruber. In 1931 Abe Troyer and Jacob Stutzman led a group out of the Swartzentruber Church. They are usually referred to as Troyer Amish.

The Swartzentrubers and Troyers use the same types of vehicles which represent the most conservative of the Ohio style. These buggies and top wagons have no windows at all. Other Ohio groups have at least a small back window. Only the small dash is permitted and no electric lights or red triangles are to be seen on these vehicles.

The Swartzentrubers are centered in Wayne County, Ohio, and adjacent Holmes County where there are twelve districts. There are also settlements at Lodi, Ohio, Freeport, Ohio, Ethridge, Tennessee, Desboro, Ontario, Canton, Minnesota, Heuvelton, New York, and Gladwin Michigan.

Most of the Troyers moved away from Holmes and Wayne Counties and now have settlements at Conewango Valley, New York, Norwich,

This street scene from Kidron, Ohio shows three vehicles common to the Swartzentruber Amish: the top buggy, the open buggy, and the heavy farm wagon.

65

The Troyer Amish top wagon from Conewango Valley, N.Y. (left), and the Swartzentruber Amish buggy from Kidron, Ohio (right) both feature the small dash and no windows.

Ontario, Lucknow, Ontario, Sugar Grove, Pennsylvania, Fryburg, Pennsylvania, and Greenville, Michigan. The Abe Miller group of Ethridge, Tennessee is a splinter from the Swartzentrubers and many of the people at Lobelville, Tennessee came from the Abe Miller group. The English, Indiana settlement is also partly composed of Swartzentruber elements.

Ohio Style Used Elsewhere

A number of Amish settlements in the Mid-west, mainly in Iowa, Missouri, and Wisconsin make use of Ohio style buggies. The oldest and largest settlement in this group is at Buchanan County, Iowa. This was a 1915 conservative offshot from Kalona, Iowa. Buchanan buggies have side and back windows, no storm front, and no electric lights. The side and back roll curtains are fastened to the inside of the buggy when not in use, thus hiding them from view. The two seat vehicle common to Buchanan County is a type of top wagon with side divider panels.

The Amish community at Bowling Green, Missouri, settled by some conservative Indiana folk, goes back to 1948. Their buggies are similar to those of Buchanan County except that the roll curtains are often fastened to the outside. The top wagons at Bowling Green do not have the side divider panels. The new settlement at Booneville, Missouri is made up of former Bowling Green people. Many people at Bowling Green are of Swiss Amish background (see pages 74-77) and some families continue the Swiss practice of using only open vehicles.

The Amish at Clark, Missouri came mainly from Buchanan County, Iowa and the vehicles are very much the same. The one difference is that the Clark buggies are usually made with masonite panels rather than top fabric. This is also the trend at Bowling Green, Missouri, McIntire, Iowa (a

Clark daughter colony) and some settlements in Wisconsin.

Cashton, Wisconsin Amish vehicles are similar to those of Bowling Green, Missouri. A new style has developed here featuring an entrance to the front only with a divided front seat that folds out of the way to allow access to the backseat.

Greenwood, Wisconsin has the Buchanan types but with outside roll curtains. The Mt. Elgin, Ontario, Granton, Wisconsin, and Utica, Minnesota Amish have Buchanan types with storm fronts. This is also true of McRae, Arkansas where surrey type vehicles are a third option. At Augusta and Wilton, Wisconsin the Buchanan style vehicles have flexible roll-up storm fronts which probably originated at Medford, Wisconsin (see Indiana section). The Huntington, Tennessee, Springville, Tennessee, and Smiley, Texas Amish settlements have nearly equal numbers of both Buchanan and Bowling Green style top wagons. At these places storm fronts are also used.

These vehicles from Mt. Elgin, Ontario originate from Buchanan County, Iowa and Clark, Missouri and are typical of a number of Midwestern Amish communities.

Ohio Style May Have Originated in Pennsylvania

In Somerset, Pennsylvania one also finds the Ohio style buggy. It is likely that this community, where Amish have lived since 1772, originated the style. There is no tradition of any other kind being used there nor memory of open buggies being used exclusively.

Sliding doors have been used in Somerset since the 1950's. The older style buggy has a full width back curtain, but a newer type with a plywood hinged door and window is becoming popular. Storm fronts and sun visors

This scene from Somerset County, Pa. shows buggies parked at one of the few Old Order Amish meetinghouses.

are usual features. Side and back windows tend to be rather large. Two seat vehicles have two sets of overlapping doors which can slide over top of each other.

Long top wagons with three front facing seats are also found in Somerset. Many of this type still have roll curtains but some three seaters have been equipped with sliding doors. Open buggies are still used by many Somerset youth.

Ohio Adaptations in Dover, Delaware

Amish from many different areas began settling at Dover, Delaware in 1915. Dover vehicles are more like those of Somerset County, Pennsylvania, and the Mid-west than those of nearby Lancaster, Pennsylvania. All Dover vehicles have sliding doors, storm fronts, sun visors, and small slide windows. A unique characteristic of Dover buggies are the sides which round toward the buggy box, instead of the usual angled-in sides.

There are several different types of vehicles in use at Dover: the single

The Dover, Delaware buggy (left) features unique rounded sides and a walk-in back door. The Arthur, Illinois buggy (right) has characteristically large windows.

seat top buggy, the two seat buggy with sliding doors in the front and a split front seat allowing access to the back seat, a two seat buggy with two sets of overlapping sliding doors; and a buggy with sliding doors for the front seat and a walk-in door at the back for two facing side seats. The first three types have plywood back panels with cut out hinged doors for the storage compartment and back window. Some examples have a short roll-up curtain for the back window.

The traditional Dover open spring wagon is called a durban. These have high side racks which extend the whole length of the wagon. A simple board resting on adjacent side boards serves as a seat. Some recent examples have more conventional upholstered seats with backrests.

Communities that are closely related to Dover and probably use the same type vehicles are LeRaysville, Pennsylvania, Andover, Ohio, Albion, Michigan, Marion, Kentucky, Muncy, Pennsylvania and Senecca Falls, New York. The Amish at St. Marys, Ontario also use similar vehicles but usually without the rounded sides.

The thirteen Amish districts around Arthur, Illinois occupy very level country. The vehicles here have a rather heavy wooden framework but the extra weight poses little problem for the horses since there are few hills. Buggies and top wagons have sliding doors and two-part storm fronts. Both of these features were introduced in the late 1930's. Rather large back and side windows are typical in Arthur. Top wagons have overlapping doors like those of Somerset and Dover. The profuse use of tacks to fasten the top fabric to the frame gives Arthur vehicles a unique look. And in that community, open spring wagons with two seats and open buggies are seen occasionally during warm weather.

Buggies similar to those of Arthur or Somerset are found at Jamesport, Missouri, Milton, Iowa, and Bloomfield, Iowa. At Jamesport surreys are the typical two seater; at the two Iowa settlements top wagons are also to be found. La Plata, Missouri Amish have mostly sliding door buggies and top wagons with divider panels. At Milton and La Plata only kerosene lights are used on the buggies.

All of the communities discussed thus far in this chapter make exclusive use of steel tires on buggy wheels. If a group uses hard rubber tires it is usually an indication that it is of a more liberal turn. This is not always true, however.

Innovations in Aylmer, Ontario Buggies

The Amish community at Aylmer, Ontario is quite conservative in matters of dress and technology but their buggies are quite innovative. The majority of the first settlers were of Daviess County, Indiana background. The Aylmer groups' use of rubber tires and breast strap harnesses reflect their Daviess background. Unlike Daviess vehicles,

Note the distinctive roof and windows on the Aylmer, Ontario buggy (left) and the ornamental cornice board on the Holmes County, Ohio New Order buggy (right).

however, most Aylmer buggies have tops, and quite unique ones at that. The typical family vehicle has a walk-in door in the back and facing side seats. Sliding doors gain access to the front seat. Windows are large. The roofs on these vehicles extend out rather far in the front and back.

An earlier type of Aylmer top wagon had side seats the whole length of the body which meant even the driver had to sit sideways. Single seat buggies are similar to those used in Somerset, Arthur and Jamesport. Other types of vehicles reflecting the varied background of the Aylmer community are also to be seen. Some Aylmer style buggies may also be found at Marshfield, Missouri and Dixon, Missouri.

The Amish at Meiserville, Pennsylvania, Norfolk, New York, and Prattsburg, New York, are largely of Swiss Amish background (pages 74-77). The majority of these people have switched from open vehicles to Ohio style buggies with sliding doors and storm fronts.

"Relaxed" Buggy Standards

Going back to Holmes County, Ohio we find fourteen districts known as New Order Amish. This group has adopted rubber tires and sliding doors on typical Holmes County vehicles.

At a number of smaller communities Ohio style buggies with rubber tires and sliding doors are the general rule. Many of these settlements have rather transient or heterogeneous populations. In most cases rigid standards on buggy details are not maintained. Therefore it is rather difficult to make general statements about these communities.

At Guthrie, Kentucky there is an active buggy shop producing vehicles for several smaller settlements. Here the buggies have a plywood back panel with a short fabric roll curtain. Oakland, Maryland also has its

The Holmes County, Ohio surrey (left) can be identified as New Order by the sliding doors. This is also a feature on Oakland, Maryland vehicles (right).

own shop but there is still considerable variety in vehicle styles. At both of these places tractors are often used for transportation and meetinghouses are used. This is also the case at Stuarts Draft, Virginia, Crofton, Kentucky, Spencer, Wisconsin, and the King Church at Hartville, Ohio. Other tractor-using communities are located at Kokomo, Indiana, Martinsburg, Ohio, Hicksville, Ohio, and Dogwood, Missouri. The Amish at Brodhead, Wisconsin, Kinsman, Ohio, Townville, Pennsylvania, Conneautville, Pennsylvania, Milroy, Indiana, West Union, Ohio, Salem, Indiana, Windsor, Missouri, Belle Center, Ohio and the larger group at Hartville, Ohio make a more limited use of tractors. The Plain City, Ohio, New Glarus, Wisconsin, and Holladay, Tennessee settlements are similar but are now on the verge of extinction.

A number of the above named communities have their own buggy shops. The Amish at Hartville and Martinsburg, Ohio get their new buggies from Holmes County. The Kokomo community had a buggy maker until recently but now get their vehicles from Arthur, Illinois.

12. Indiana

As in Ohio, the Amish in north central Indiana formerly used only open buggies. Tops began appearing in the early 1900's. The pattern chosen was different from the Ohio style in that the top extended only to the seat of the buggy and not over the "boot" or storage compartment in the rear. On both buggies and surreys the top fabric extends only to the seat edge rather than to the box. This type of construction is found in Iowa, Kansas, Oklahoma, Wisconsin and a number of other areas in addition to Indiana.

In some new communities both the Indiana and Ohio style buggies will be seen. When such a mixture occurs the Ohio style usually wins out because of its more efficient use of space (see sketches on page 45).

The level country in north central Indiana is the home of the third largest Amish community: the adjoining settlements in La Grange County and Elkhart County. These groups have always maintained their separate identities since they were founded in the 1840's. Both groups use the Indiana shape buggy but in La Grange they have the roll-up side curtains while in Elkhart sliding doors have become common. Surreys are the predominate two-seat vehicle and are seen more frequently during the week than in Holmes County. Steel tires are the rule in La Grange but rubber tires are permitted in Elkhart. Both groups have storm fronts.

In La Grange County the trend toward larger side windows and two

These are the two most common types of vehicles found in La Grange County, Indiana. The buggy (left) has one seat; the surrey (right) has two seats.

back windows has developed in the last fifteen years. The old style small dashboard was used here into the 1940's and about the same time divider panels on the sides of surreys began to appear. Headlights on La Grange buggies are small and mounted on the dash. Cab wagons are very common in this area but two-wheeled carts have only been common for a few years.

Close by to the south of Elkhart and La Grange Counties is the equally old Amish settlement at Nappanee, Indiana. Of the sixteen districts here all but two have accepted sliding doors, rubber tires, and breast strap harnesses. These innovations came in the 1960's. At Centerville, Michigan these new items are occasionally seen but most vehicles are like those of La Grange County. The new settlements at Kingston, Wisconsin, and Hale, Michigan follow the La Grange pattern while at Charlotte, Michigan the Elkhart-Nappanee trend is most common.

Style Spread to Kansas

Like Elkhart and La Grange the Amish community near Hutchinson, Kansas actually consists of two side-by-side settlements. Similarly, the Amish near Partridge, Kansas have accepted more innovations than those of Haven, Kansas. At Partridge rubber tires are used but at Haven they are not. The Partridge people also make use of bicycles and tractors for transportation while the Haven people do not. The Amish at Garnette, Kansas and Chouteau, Oklahoma are similar to those of Partridge. All these communities make use of the Indiana style vehicles but have sliding side curtains on their buggies and surreys. This style pulls down somewhat like a window blind. This type of curtain is also used by a minority of people in Elkhart County, Indiana, Kokomo, Indiana, Jamesport, Missouri, Belle

The Nappanee, Indiana buggy and surrey shown here feature sliding doors and large windows. Note the breast strap harness (left) and rubber tires.

Center, Ohio, Plain City, Ohio, and probably in a few other places.

These sliding curtains have been the general rule at Kalona, Iowa since the late 1940's. Here the buggies are much the same as the Indiana style but the top is somewhat narrower and not as square. The Kalona surreys have a narrow divider panel along the sides or none at all. A third

This Kalona, Iowa buggy has side curtains which slide down, somewhat like a window blind.

type of vehicle at Kalona is used for hauling purposes and resembles a long Ohio style top wagon with sliding doors.

Roll-Up Storm Fronts

Another area where the Indiana style buggy is used is Medford, Wisconsin. This settlement was founded in 1925 largely by Amish from Kansas. The Medford people are perhaps the most conservative to use the Indiana style buggy. The unique storm fronts are made of flexible material and can be rolled up like a side curtain. The Buchanan style top wagon with side divider panels is the common two-seat vehicle. Related settlements at Amherst, Blair, and Chetek, Wisconsin and Bertha and Wadena, Minnesota use the same types of vehicles as Medford but surreys may also be found at some of these places.

Indiana type vehicles are used in a number of newer settlements where there has been a blending of people using both the Indiana and the

Ohio styles. Those places where a significant number use the Indiana style are Anabel, Missouri (Medford type), Bronson, Michigan (La Grange type), Mio, Michigan, Spencer, Wisconsin, Rexford, Montana, Clarita, Oklahoma, Bloomfield, Iowa, Belle Center, Ohio, and Hicksville, Ohio (Elkhart, Nappanee, and Kalona types).

This Haven, Kansas buggy is no doubt owned by a creative youth. Two horses are used to pull the Medford, Wisconsin top wagon.

13. Swiss

Most Old Order Amish are descended from immigrants that arrived in America in the eighteenth century. A separate wave of Amish migration from Europe occurred in the nineteenth century. The majority of these latecomers eventually lost their Amish identity; however, a few groups remained in the Old Order.

Today these people are recognized as a distinct minority among the Amish. They are generally referred to as Swiss Amish because their dialect is related to that of Berne, Switzerland rather than the German Palatinate related Pennsylvania German. Since they were isolated from their American brethren for about a century the Swiss developed somewhat different customs and practices. This applies to dress, singing, church order, and vehicles.

These Berne, Indiana shoppers have come to town in a two-seat wagon with no top.

Only Open Buggies Used

All the Swiss communities use open vehicles exclusively. Other Amish may make frequent use of buggies and wagons with no tops but the Swiss are restricted to these alone. It has been mentioned that other midwestern Amish had this same custom earlier in the century.

One might think that riding in a buggy with no top would be

unbearably cold in the winter. One open buggy driver pointed out that a snow mobile is considerably more breezy than a buggy. It must also be remembered that sleighs very seldom had tops. Large umbrellas are generally standard equipment on Swiss vehicles.

The community in Adams County around Berne, Indiana is the largest, most conservative, and most ethnically Swiss of the four major Swiss settlements. The common vehicle here is very simple in design and about midway in size between a buggy and a spring wagon. These buggies may be descended from the Concord wagon which also shared the Adams County characteristic of long half-eliptic springs stretching from axle to axle. In Adams County other arrangements of half-eliptic springs are seen, but never the front and back eliptics so common elsewhere. Many of the long springs are salvaged from junked autos.

No Backrests

Adams County buggies have very high dashes but no backrests, often called "lazy backs," on the seats. The seats are padded with a folded blanket and not upholstered. Blinker lights and red triangles are permitted but lanterns are still preferred over electric lights.

When a young man begins his family, the front and back storage compartment doors are removed on his buggy to make room for children. When the family gets larger (twelve or more children are quite common Adams County) an extra seat or two on the long bedded "Johnny wagon" may suffice. Two-wheeled carts are occasionally seen in Adams County.

Adams County buggies are also found at Seymour, Missouri and Reading, Michigan.

In general appearance the vehicles used in Allen County, Indiana near Fort Wayne are similar to those of Adams County. The main common feature is the lack of a backrest. Allen buggies are smaller, have an exceptionally nice paint job, an upholstered seat, eliptic springs, and are

The Adams County, Indiana buggy (left) is of a simpler design than the Allen County, Indiana buggy (right). Both communities do not allow tops or backrests.

often seen with a profusion of reflectors and ornamental tacks. The dashboards have an outward curve at the top edge which is finished with an ornamental cut-out design. Two-seated vehicles in Allen County are of the surrey type. Electric headlights are standard.

Allen County people are also found at Quincy, Michigan and South Whitley, Indiana. The Camden and Homer, Michigan settlements are also of Allen County background but are more conservative. The Amish at Hamilton, Indiana are a mixture of Allen and Adams folk.

As was mentioned in the Ohio section many people of Swiss background live at Bowling Green, Missouri, Meiserville, Pennsylvania, Norfolk, New York, and Prattsburg, New York but top buggies are predominate at these places.

A Daviess County, Indiana boy elaborately decorated this auto seat buggy.

Borrowings from Larger Society

In Daviess County, Indiana the Amish have kept the Swiss custom of open buggies but have adopted some innovations which were common in the larger American society in the early 1900's. The gracefully curving "auto seat" style is typical here. These were patterned after early horseless carriage models. Currently the seats are often molded from fiberglass. Rubber tires and breast strap harnesses are also common to Daviess. Very high plywood dashboards have nearly replaced the smaller traditional type leather dashes. Spring wagons sometimes called "long

Johns" can be equipped with one or more back seats. The example pictured is a highly decorated version owned by a young boy. Most buggies are not this elaborate.

The Amish settlement around Milverton, Ontario is generally not considered Swiss but the people here are descended from nineteenth century European immigrants. The open buggies have seats with simple straight backrests. The dashboards are rather elaborate affairs made of artificial leather sewn to a metal framework. These were first seen in the larger society shortly before World War I. Spring wagons double as two-seat vehicles. Breast strap harnesses predominate but only steel tires are allowed.

The back seat of the Daviess County "long john" may be removed for hauling space. Milverton, Ontario buggies feature elaborate leather dashes.

14. Old Order Mennonites

Although the Amish are recognized as the most conservative branch of the Mennonite family tree, there are Mennonites who are equally and, in some cases, more conservative than some of the less traditional Amish. These people are referred to collectively as Old Order Mennonites but the origins of the various groups among them are rather diverse.

During the last half of the nineteenth century many innovations were being introduced into the Mennonite church. Many conservative minded members withdrew from the larger body and formed independent groups. This process took place between 1845 and 1901 in Pennsylvania, Ontario, Indiana, Ohio, and Virginia. New points of dissension arose at all these places in the twentieth century and the Old Order Mennonites divided into automobile and horse and buggy groups.

Four geographical groups of Old Order Mennonites form the largest ecclesiastical unit among these people. The largest of these is the Groffdale Conference often referred to as Wenger Mennonites. The others are centered at Waterloo County, Ontario, Dayton, Virginia, and Wakarusa, Indiana. Customs and practices vary from one community to the next. This is especially true in regard to buggies. Smaller, usually more conservative groups are located in most of the older communities.

More than 14,000 Mennonites (including children) in North America drive horses and buggies. In fact in Lancaster County, Pa. half as many Mennonites use horse-drawn vehicles as Amish do.

The Wenger Mennonites are concentrated in northern Lancaster County, Pennsylvania. Other churches have been established in Pennsylvania at Kutztown, Mifflinburg, Shippensburg, and Martinsburg. New Wenger settlements have also been started at Barnette, Missouri, Shiloh, Ohio, Thorp, Wisconsin, Penn Yann, New York, and Liberty, Kentucky. There are currently over 3,000 members.

Black Buggies for Wenger Mennonites

The typical Wenger Mennonite family carriage has two seats and a black straight-sided top. The box tapers in at the back and sides. Large plexiglass windows in the sliding doors first appeared about 1960 and have now largely replaced the old style with small windows. Before sliding doors were introduced roll curtains were attached to a hinged metal frame which could be opened like a door when the curtain was down. Storm fronts and sun visors are standard and newer vehicles have hydraulic brakes. Shorter versions of the carriage with only one seat are used by some old people. A few young men have also adopted a rather deluxe version of this style.

The Wenger Mennonite spring wagon shown here is black. Many others have a green box and yellow wheels. Most Wenger Mennonite youth prefer folding top buggies.

Folding Tops on Young Men's Buggies

Buggies with folding or falling tops are favored by Wenger young people. In warm weather the tops are tilted back partway but are seldom folded back completely. Snap-on side curtains are in place more often than not. A type of storm front is attached to the ceiling when not in use. Rectangular dashes made of artificial leather sewn to a metal framework are common to Wenger buggies. Young folks often decorate their buggies with elaborate pin striping, decals, reflecting tape and reflectors.

Yellow and Green Spring Wagons

Open buggies are a rarity but there are two types of open spring wagons. The difference is in color rather than construction. In addition to the common black variety there are a large number of wagons with yellow running gear and green boxes. This was a frequent color combination when such wagons were mass produced.

Top wagons are rare among the Wengers. A few examples are especially designed to facilitate wheel chairs. Two-wheeled carts are very common and cab wagons are beginning to appear.

Collar harnesses and steel tires are still predominant among the Wengers.

The two groups of Reidenbach or "Thirty-fiver Mennonites" in Lancaster County, though more conservative otherwise, have vehicles identical to those of the Wengers.

The Pike Mennonites, named for their meetinghouse on the "Pike" (Route 322) in Lancaster County, are the oldest and most conservative of the Old Order Mennonites. Since their origin in 1845 they have suffered

These are vehicles of the Pike Mennonites, the most conservative of Old Order Mennonites. There are no back or side windows, but a storm front is allowed.

numerous divisions. The largest group is the Stauffer Mennonite Church which has congregations in Lancaster County and Snyder County, Pennsylvania (near Port Trevorton), Leonardtown, Maryland, and Tunas, Missouri. There are about four hundred members.

The most characteristic feature of Stauffer vehicles is the lack of windows on the back, sides, and sliding doors. Storm fronts are allowed however. The carriages have two seats and square cornered boxes. A few one-seat carriages exist. Long bodied top wagons often have facing side seats in the back. Open buggies with no dashboards are common to young people. Stauffers allow battery blinker lights but otherwise only gasoline or kerosene lanterns are used.

The smaller Weaver group in Lancaster County allows sliding doors with large windows but no back windows. They also have battery headlights. The Noah Hoover group has now largely relocated in Scottsville, Kentucky from Snyder County, Pennsylvania. A Hoover settlement is also located at Monterey, Tennessee. Formerly most of the Hoovers used open spring wagons as their main type of vehicle but now older style Wenger-type carriages with small windows are permitted. A number of other Pike groups in Snyder County have carriages like those of the Stauffers.

Virginians Salvage Antiques

It has been said that among the Rockingham County, Virginia Old Order Mennonites no two buggies are exactly alike. This characteristic is largely due to the fact that most vehicles are salvaged antiques. Folding top buggies with four top bows, side curtains, and auto seats are the most common general type. Various kinds of two-seat folding top surreys and phaetons are also commonly seen. Newer styles of vehicles with stationary tops and sliding doors are beginning to replace the renovated antiques. The single seat variety is called a "squarey" or "box buggy." Rubber tires

The Mennonites of Dayton, Virginia have made use of rather elaborate vehicles leftover from the larger society.

and breast strap harnesses are used by most of the Virginia Old Orders.

Indiana Mennonites Adapt Other Styles

The Virginia style box buggy has largely replaced the falling top buggies for the Wakarusa, Indiana Mennonite young folks. Indiana two-seat vehicles have a surrey style fiberglass box and sliding doors for the front seats similar to a Pennsylvania style arrangement. Side windows are rather large and there are usually two back windows.

Open Buggies in Ontario

The majority of Old Order Mennonites in Waterloo County, Ontario

The square top buggy (left) has largely replaced the folding top buggy among Wakarusa, Indiana Mennonite youth. The vehicle at right is the typical family buggy.

use only open vehicles. The single seat buggies have either a standard straight seat or a fancier auto seat. The latter is preferred by young people. Both types have elaborate artificial leather dashes with loops in the upper corners.

Some long-bodied spring wagons have three full seats but more commonly a backward facing bench-like seat is placed between the front and back seat when it is needed for children. Even the back seat can be removed during the week to allow room for hauling space.

Unlike their Amish neighbors at Milverton the Mennonites make occasional use of top buggies. These never were too popular and are largely used by older people.

Rubber tires are found on the vehicles of the largest Mennonite groups in Waterloo County but three smaller groups do not allow them. One of these smaller churches, the David Martin group, make frequent use of two-wheeled carts, a practice not common among Ontario Old Orders. Unlike the Wenger Mennonites the Ontario Old Order Mennonites rarely make use of bicycles and not at all on Sunday.

The now extinct Old Order Mennonite community at Brutus,

Most Old Order Mennonites of Waterloo County, Ontario use only open vehicles. Like Old Order Mennonites in other parts of North America, they worship in simple meetinghouses.

Despite manifold difficulties and hardships, these people choose the warmth of community and disciplined living instead of the convenience of modern mobility, luxury and rootlessness.

Michigan began in 1879. The settlers were mainly from Ontario and Indiana. A controversy erupted in the 1920's when those of Indiana background wanted to adopt top buggies which was contrary to Ontario tradition. A temporary split occurred but an understanding was reached and top buggies did gain acceptance.

15. Other Groups

German Baptists

The religious movement started by Alexander Mack in 1708 at Schwarzenau, Germany, has variously been known as Brethren, German Baptist, Dunkers, and numerous combinations and variations of these three names. The largest traditional faction of this movement took the name Old German Baptist Brethren after their 1881 division with the majority group now known as the Church of the Brethren.

In the early twentieth century two small ultraconservative elements withdrew from the Old German Baptist Brethren. The one group now known as Old Brethren German Baptists date to 1913 and is centered at Carrol County, Indiana, Wakarusa, Indiana and Mammoth Springs, Arkansas. The other group originated in 1921 and took the name Old Order German Baptist. They live mainly in Darke County, Ohio and neighboring Miami County.

Both groups continue to use horse-drawn vehicles but the Old Order German Baptists allow tractors while the Old Brethren German Baptists do not. Most of the vehicles used by both groups are largely remnants from the larger American society built just before the total domination by autos. The typical single seat buggies were once known as storm buggies or cozy cabs. With ample glass windows and sliding doors which can also be traced to non-plain manufacturers are the typical two-seat vehicles found among German Baptists. Most vehicles have solid rubber tires. Some of these people are beginning to make use of new and used Amish built vehicles. Most buggy repair and harness work is done in Amish shops.

The Old Order German Baptists have made use of vehicles salvaged from those used by the larger society at the end of the buggy era.

A small number of Old Order River Brethren in Franklin County, Pa. still make use of horse-drawn vehicles.

Old Order River Brethren

The River Brethren originated along the Susquehanna River in Lancaster County, Pennsylvania, about 1780. The first members were mostly former Mennonites that were highly influenced by the German Baptist Brethren and the revivalistic forerunners of the United Brethren. Supposedly in the mid-1850's the traditional element withdrew from the moderate majority. The traditionalists took the name Old Order River Brethren; the moderates, Brethren in Christ. The former group is often referred to as Yorker Brethren since many of the first members came from York County, Pennsylvania.

Beginning in 1920 a series of divisions wreaked havoc among the Old Order River Brethren. In 1980 after two mergers the total was reduced to three groups. Only one of the groups currently makes use of horse-drawn vehicles. This fellowship is concentrated in Franklin County, Pennsylvania where there are about forty members. Two Lancaster County groups used horses until 1951 and 1954 respectively. A third Lancaster group had buggies until about 1960.

Old Order River Brethren carriages are similar to those of the Pike and Wenger Mennonites. In fact in recent years vehicles have been obtained directly from the Wenger Mennonites.

Common features on Yorker carriages are sliding doors with small windows or no windows, storm fronts, sun visors, and solid rubber tires. Jumpseats were often utilized which made it possible to change a single seat carriage to a two seater.

Old Colony Mennonites

Northern Mexico may seem an unlikely place to find plain people but, nonetheless, the second largest Old Order group is located there. People known as Old Colony Mennonites occupy large tracts in the state of Chihuahua near Cuatemoc and Casas Grandes and in Durango.

These German-speaking people emigrated from Manitoba and Saskatchewan in western Canada in the 1920's. They came to North America in the 1870's from Russia. The name, "Old Colony," derives from their origin at Chortitza, the oldest Mennonite settlement in Russia. The Russian settlers were originally from Prussia and the Prussian Mennonites can be traced to Holland. So, the Old Colony group represents the Old Order element of Dutch Mennonitism, a separate branch from the Swiss Mennonites from which the Amish and Old Order Mennonites descend. The Old Colony Mennonites emerged as a distinct group in the 1880's in Manitoba.

This is the style of buggy originally used by the Old Colony Mennonites in Mexico.

According to Harry Leonard Sawatzky's study, **They Sought a Country**, the Old Colony people in Mexico have retained horse-drawn vehicles. The more progressive Old Colonies who have remained in Canada or emigrated to Canada and the United States from Mexico have all accepted autos. The Ft. Vermillion settlement in Alberta was one of the last Canadian groups to give up horses.

Large groups have left the Mexican settlements in the last few decades and established themselves in Belize, Bolivia, and Paraguay. This last emigration largely represents the ultra-conservative element among the Old Colonies. It may well be that horse-drawn vehicles will survive longest in these areas.

When the Mennonites arrived in Mexico they brought with them conventional buggies and wagons. When the Canadian Old Colonies gave up horse travel around World War II the Mexicans quickly bought up their buggies. These wooden wheeled vehicles are still seen in Mexico and presumably in the other Latin American settlements but a cheaper and more easily maintained vehicle has become more popular.

Discarded automobiles could be had in abundance in Mexico beginning in the 1930's. The Mennonites stripped these down to their bare chassis and converted them to practical two-horse wagons with pneumatic tires. These "Karrenwagen" (auto-wagons) can be used as utility vehicles or equipped with tops and roll curtains or trailer-like cabs with large windows. The Mennonites in Durango favor lighter weight

Most Old Colony Mennonites now use "Karren wagon" which are made on old auto chassis. The man at left manufactures these vehicles.

versions of the Karrenwagen which can be pulled by one horse.

Two communities in the Central American country of Belize located at Upper and Lower Barton Creek are made up of diverse elements. Many came from the Kleine Gemeinde Mennonites, a Russian group, and various other groups of American origin. They are very conservative and are independent of any other Old Order groups.

Glossary

APRON — A protective canvas shield used for weather protection on open front vehicles.

AUTO SEAT — A style of buggy seat modeled after early automobiles of the 1900's.

AXLE — The axis on which the wheel revolves. May be of three different types: straight, arch-curved upward, or drop-curved downward. A wooden cap is often attached to the top of the axle.

BOB SLED — A heavy sled usually with two sets of runners.

BODY HANGER — The curved pieces of steel used to attach the buggy body to the eliptic springs. This style favored in the Mid-west. Also called a body loop but different from the style described below.

BODY LOOP — The metal bracket which attaches the buggy body to the spring bar. The predominant style in Pennsylvania.

BOOT — The small storage compartment in the back of a buggy.

BORIUM — A substance made of tungsten-carbide particles welded to horseshoes for traction.

BOX — The bottom part of the vehicle body. May also refer to the seat.

BUGGY — Usually associated with a one-seat vehicle with or without a top. In many cases may refer to any non-utility vehicle.

CAB WAGON — The author's term for a light utility vehicle with an enclosed front and an open bed.

CARRIAGE — Among plain people this term is used primarily in Pennsylvania to refer to a two-seat vehicle with a top.

COLLAR — The part of the harness which bears the weight of the vehicle. The round collar fits around the horse's neck; the breast collar consists of a wide band encircling the horse's chest.

CURTAIN — The fabric covering for the sides and back of a vehicle. This writer uses the term only for the parts that can be rolled up.

CUTTER — A lightweight sleigh usually with one seat.

DASH or DASHBOARD — The protective panel on the front of a vehicle.

DRILL-TEC — Small particles of ground-up drill bits welded to horseshoes for traction.

DRIVING HORSE — A horse used to pull a passenger vehicle.

EXTENSION TOP — A vehicle top which may be folded down.

FALLING TOP — The same as an extension top.

FARRIER — One who shoes horses; often called a blacksmith.

FIFTH WHEEL — The turning device attached to the front axle of a vehicle.

FLASHER LIGHTS — Red or amber battery-operated lights attached to buggies which flash on and off as a caution signal for motorists. Required by law in many states.

HEAD BLOCK — The wooden piece between the spring and the fifth wheel on a vehicle.

MARKET WAGON — An enclosed utility vehicle often used with two seats. This term is most often used in Pennsylvania.

MUD SPLASHER — A canvas shield hanging between the cross piece of the shafts and the buggy axle.

OLD ORDER — In this book, used to refer to people maintaining horse-drawn travel. In a wider sense, some groups that use cars but have preserved a traditional form of worship are considered Old Order.

OPEN — Used in reference to a vehicle without a top or storm front.

PACER — A horse trained to have a gait in which both legs on the same side are raised at the same time.

PERCH — The long rectangular pieces connecting the front and back axles. May be single or double. Also called a reach.

PLAIN PEOPLE — Those religious groups that have preserved a simple traditional lifestyle, especially distinctive dress.

POLE — The single extension from a vehicle which is used to facilitate the use of two horses. Also called a tongue.

REACH — See PERCH.

RIG — The combination of a horse and vehicle.

RUNNING GEAR — The wheels, axles, fifth wheel, head block, perches, and springs of a vehicle. Also called the under-carriage.

SADDLEBRED or AMERICAN SADDLE HORSE — A breed of horse often trained as a driving horse.

SHAFTS — The two long projections from the vehicle axle between which the horse stands and to which parts of the harness are attached.

SIDE DIVIDER PANEL — The permanent panel on the side of a two-seat vehicle in line with the front seat.

SIDE PANEL — The stationary rear side curtains of a vehicle.

SINGLE TREE — The movable wooden bar on the shaft cross-piece to which the traces are attached. Also called a whiffle tree.

SLOW-MOVING VEHICLE TRIANGLE — A luminous red triangle required by law in many states as a safety warning symbol for horse-drawn vehicles.

SPRINGS — Eliptic leaf springs are most commonly used on the front and back of light vehicles. Two such springs are used for each wheel on heavier vehicles. Duplex springs, platform springs, and telegraph springs are various arrangements of half eliptic springs which afford extra suspension on the rear of vehicles. Concord or long springs running length-wise are common to Adams County, Indiana.

SPRING BAR — Used in combination with body loops to attach the vehicle to the springs. Usually made of wood.

SPRING WAGON — A term usually referring to an open utility vehicle. Often used to describe a two-seat vehicle with a top which this writer calls a top wagon.

STANDARDBRED — A breed of horse developed for light harness use.

STORM FRONT — A protective windshield of glass or any other clear substance on the front of a vehicle.

SURREY — A two seat vehicle with a sloping front floor board and a back seat which projects outward from the box. Does not necessarily have a "fringe on the top."

TAXI — A hired car or van. Not necessarily part of a company.

TEAM — Two or more horses used together. In Pennsylvania used to refer to the combination of a horse and vehicle.

TIRE — The steel or rubber rims on the outside of a wheel.

TOP WAGON — A long vehicle with a top used with two seats or as a utility. Usually has extra suspension on the rear axle. Heavier and less elaborate than a surrey.

TRACES — The long leather straps attaching the single tree to the horse collar. The means by which the vehicle is pulled.

TROTTER — A horse that travels with its feet lifted in alternate diagonal pairs.

UNDER-CARRIAGE — See RUNNING GEAR.

WHIFFLE-TREE — See SINGLE TREE.

WHIP SOCKET — The holder for the whip on a vehicle.

Readings and Sources
Old Order Life and History

Allgyer, John D. *Kentucky Bound*. Pequea Publishers, Gordonville, Pennsylvania, 1981. Two Amish men travel 970 miles in a covered wagon.

Anon. "The Amish of Lancaster County, Pennsylvania," *The Pennsylvania German*, XII, #6 (June, 1911). An early 20th century look at the Amish.

Benedict, Fred W. "The Old Orders and Schism," *Brethren Life and Thought*, XVIII, #1 (Winter 1973), 25–32. A survey of the groups related to the Old German Baptists.

Burkholder, Anna. *Daniel S. Burkholder Family History*. Amos B. Hoover, Denver, Pennsylvania, 1981. Contains some good accounts of issues which affected the Old Order Mennonites.

Cronk, Sandra. "Gelassenheit: The Rites of the Redemptive Process in Old Order Amish and Old Order Mennonite Communities," *Mennonite Quarterly Review*, LV, #1 (January 1981), 5–44. An excellent explanation of the Old Order way of life.

Good, Merle and Phyllis. *Twenty Most Asked Questions About the Amish and Mennonites*. Good Books, Lancaster, Pennsylvania, 1979. An introduction to the distinctive beliefs and practices of the plain people.

Hoover, Amos. "The Old Order Mennonites," *Mennonite World Handbook*. Mennonite World Conference, Lombard, Illinois, 1978, 374–381. The best survey of the various Old Order Mennonite groups written by one of their own people.

Horst, Isaac R. *Separate and Peculiar*. Isaac R. Horst, Mt. Forest, Ontario, 1979. A detailed account of Canadian Old Order Mennonite life written in story form.

Hostetler, John A. *Amish Society*. Johns Hopkins University Press, Baltimore, Maryland, 1980 (Third edition). The most thorough account of Amish life.

Kurtz, John S. "The Automobile Issue among the Old Order Mennonites: 1920," *Mennonite Historical Bulletin*, XXXVII (October 1976), 5–6. A letter written by one church leader to another.

Luthy, David. "Old Records," *Family Life*. December, 1980. Writings of two Amishmen reminiscing about the old days.

Redekop, Calvin. *The Old Colony Mennonites*. Johns Hopkins University Press, Baltimore, Maryland, 1969. A sociological study of this Latin American group.

Sawatzky, Harry Leonard. *They Sought a Country*. University of California Press, Berkeley, California, 1971. A detailed description of the Old Colony Mennonites and other groups who found a home south of the border.

Scott, Stephen. "The Old Order River Brethren," *Pennsylvania Mennonite Heritage*, I, #3 (July 1978), 13–22. An overview of Old Order River Brethren history and distinctive beliefs.

Stoll, Elmo. *One Way Street*. Pathway Publishers, Aylmer, Ontario, 1972. An Amish boy's struggle with the temptation to join a modern church.

Umble, John. "Memories of an Amish Bishop," *Mennonite Quarterly Review*, XXII (1948), 94–116. An Amish leader reflects on how things used to be.

Wagler, David. *Are All the Things Lawful?* Pathway Publishers, Aylmer, Ontario. A tract presenting the principles for using horse-drawn vehicles.

General History of the Plain People

Brumbaugh, Martin G. *History of the German Baptist Brethren*. Brethren Publishing House, Mount Morris, Illinois, 1899. Reprinted 1907, 1961, 1971. A basic history of the groups stemming from the 1708 Alexander Mack movement.

Denlinger, A. Martha. *Real People.* Herald Press, Scottdale, Pennsylvania, 1975. A comparison of the various plain groups in Lancaster County.

Dyck, Cornelius J., ed. *An Introduction to Mennonite History.* Herald Press, Scottdale, Pennsylvania, 1967. A good place to start in studying Mennonite and Amish History.

Gibbons, Phebe Earle. *Pennsylvania Dutch and other Essays.* J. B. Lippincott and Co., Philadelphia, Pennsylvania, 1882. Contains 19th century descriptions of the Amish.

Guide to Research in Brethren History. Church of the Brethren General Board, Elgin, Illinois, 1977. A pamphlet giving the basic sources for Brethren history.

Krahn, Cornelius and Gingerich, Melvin. *The Mennonites, A Brief Guide to Information,* Faith and Life Press, Newton, Kansas, 1976. A pamphlet giving an outline of Mennonite history and bibliography.

Kraybill, Paul N. *Mennonite World Handbook.* Mennonite World Conference, Lombard, Illinois, 1978. Region by region survey of diverse Mennonite and Amish groups.

Mennonite Encyclopedia, The. Herald Press, Scottdale, Pennsylvania, 1959. A four volume set covering many aspects of Mennonite and Amish history, life, and doctrine.

Wenger, John C. *The Mennonite Church in America.* Herald Press, Scottdale, Pennsylvania, 1966. Records the early history and expansion of the Mennonites and Amish.

Wittlinger, Carlton O. *Quest for Piety and Obedience.* Evangel Press, Nappanee, Indiana, 1978. A well written account of River Brethren and Brethren in Christ history.

Antique Vehicles

Berkebile, Don H. *American Carriages, Sleighs, Sulkies and Carts.* Dover Publications, New York, New York, 1977. Pictures of a variety of horse-drawn vehicles with notes as to their history.

Berkebile, Don H. *Carriage Terminology.* Smithsonian Institute, Washington, D.C., 1978. An abundance of information on vehicles and their paraphernalia based upon 19th century sources.

Rittenhouse, Jack D. *American Horse-Drawn Vehicles.* Floyd Clymer Publications, Los Angeles, California, 1948.

Horses

Brumbaugh, Owen. *Training the Buggy Horse and Training the Driver.* Horse Book Publisher, Camden, Indiana, 1981. An Old Order tells how to break bad habits of man and beast.

Davis, Lloyd H. *Keeping a Horse in the Suburbs,* Stephen Green Press, Brattleboro, Vermont, 1976. A good introduction to what is involved in taking care of a horse.

Kellogg, Charles W. *Driving the Horse in Harness.* Stephen Green Press, Brattleboro, Vermont, 1978. An excellent introduction to horses, harness, vehicles, and driving.

Morris, Pamela. *The Book of the Horse.* Putnam, New York, 1979. A large format book dealing with many facets of horsedom.

Magazines

American Horseman. Country Wide Publications, 257 Park Ave. S., New York, New York. A general interest publication on horses.

The Budget. Budget Publishing Company, Sugarcreek, Ohio. A weekly newspaper with many folksy letters from Old Order communities. Many horse and buggy related ads.

Carriage Journal. The Carriage Association, Portland, Maine. A quarterly dealing with the history of horse-drawn vehicles.

Family Life. Pathway Publishing House, Aylmer, Ontario. A monthly magazine published by Old Order Amish. As the title suggests there is something for the whole family.

Index

The Author

Stephen E. Scott grew up between Dayton and Xenia, Ohio. He first came to Lancaster County, Pennsylvania at age fourteen as part of a vacation trip with his parents. He had read about the plain people at his local library in Dayton, Ohio and persuaded his family to include the Pennsylvania Dutch land in their tour. Steve was deeply impressed by the simple godly life of the Amish, Mennonites and Brethren and began to look deeper into their faith. He lived, worked and worshiped with a number of plain groups after leaving the Baptist Church. He eventually affiliated with the Old Order River Brethren Church in 1969 in Lancaster County.

Steve studied at Cedarville (Ohio) College. He has been a school teacher and has avidly collected data about the various plain peoples. He made maps and historical charts for the **Holmes County, Ohio** and **Geauga County, Ohio Amish Directories.** He researched, drew, and published the map, "Plain Churches and Related Groups of Lancaster County, Pennsylvania." His articles have appeared in **The Diary** and **Pennsylvania Mennonite Heritage.**

Steve married Harriet Sauder in 1973. The Scotts have two children, Andrew and Hannah, and live near Columbia, Pennsylvania. Together, Steve and Harriet publish a **Church Directory of the Old Order River Brethren.**

Information for **Plain Buggies** was gathered over a period of fifteen years. Steve visited many of the Old Order communities to collect information and pictures firsthand and sent questionnaires to buggy shop proprietors and dozens of members of Old Order fellowships. In addition he researched extensively in the Old Order Amish Historical Library of Aylmer, Ontario.